The Art of Communication in Nursing and Health Care

Theresa Raphael-Grimm, PhD, CNS, holds a joint appointment as clinical associate professor in the Schools of Nursing and Medicine as well as an adjunct appointment as associate professor of psychiatry at the University of North Carolina–Chapel Hill (UNC-CH). Dr. Raphael-Grimm is a doctorate-trained psychotherapist (and nurse) who has studied clinician–patient relationships since 1986. She has been a practicing psychotherapist since 1984 and has worked with a variety of patient populations, including those with chronic and terminal illness. She also provides psychotherapy to nurses, physicians, and other clinicians. She is the facilitator for UNC-CH School of Medicine's Schwartz Center Rounds, which is a multidisciplinary exploration of psychosocial issues that impact patient care and influence clinician compassion. Dr. Raphael-Grimm has been a member of the Department of Psychiatry consult team, and worked with the UNC-CH's Comprehensive Cancer Support Program. She has delivered more than 40 invited clinical presentations at local, state, and national meetings and is a member of Sigma Theta Tau (STT) International and the American Psychological Association.

The Art of Communication in Nursing and Health Care

An Interdisciplinary Approach

Theresa Raphael-Grimm, PhD, CNS

SPRINGER PUBLISHING COMPANY

NEW YORK

Springer Publishing Company, LLC
11 West 42nd Street
New York, NY 10036
www.springerpub.com

Acquisitions Editor: Margaret Zuccarini
Composition: S4Carlisle Publishing Services

ISBN: 978-0-8261-1055-8
e-book ISBN: 978-0-8261-1056-5

16 17 / 5 4

The author and the publisher of this Work have made every effort to use sources believed to be reliable to provide information that is accurate and compatible with the standards generally accepted at the time of publication. Because medical science is continually advancing, our knowledge base continues to expand. Therefore, as new information becomes available, changes in procedures become necessary. We recommend that the reader always consult current research and specific institutional policies before performing any clinical procedure. The author and publisher shall not be liable for any special, consequential, or exemplary damages resulting, in whole or in part, from the readers' use of, or reliance on, the information contained in this book. The publisher has no responsibility for the persistence or accuracy of URLs for external or third-party Internet Web sites referred to in this publication and does not guarantee that any content on such Web sites is, or will remain, accurate or appropriate.

Library of Congress Cataloging-in-Publication Data

Raphael-Grimm, Theresa, author.
  The art of communication in nursing and health care : an interdisciplinary approach/ Theresa Raphael-Grimm.
     p. ; cm.
  Includes bibliographical references.
  ISBN 978-0-8261-1055-8—ISBN 0-8261-1055-X—ISBN 978-0-8261-1056-5 (e-book)
  I. Title.
     [DNLM: 1. Nurse–Patient Relations—Nurses' Instruction. 2. Communication—Nurses' Instruction. 3. Interpersonal Relations—Nurses' Instruction. 4. Mindfulness—Nurses' Instruction. WY 88]
  RT86.3
  610.7306'99—dc23

                                    2014021436

Printed in the United States of America by Gasch Printing.

This book is dedicated to
Rita Maria Robinson Raphael
1928–2010
whose compassion, steadfast and deep,
is woven into the fabric of my soul.

Contents

Contents

Preface

*H*ealth care delivery is complex and scientifically grounded, and requires its practitioners to possess considerable knowledge and expertise. As the science continues to advance, clinicians are expected to master ever-growing bodies of evidence-based knowledge. With so much of the focus on the scientific base of clinical practice, the *art* of patient care often gets short shrift. Yet it is the art of care that provides a deep sense of meaning and value for patients and providers alike. This book guides the reader through a conceptual framework for building effective patient relationships. Based on concepts of mindfulness, it provides a kind of mental scaffolding or operating platform on which to build thoughts, perspectives, and skills that help the busy clinician to achieve inner composure, attain greater self-awareness, and develop critical interpersonal skills that result in satisfying and compassionate patient care.

In the first section of the book, mindfulness principles are embedded in discussions of the critical elements of interpersonal effectiveness, such as hope, empathy, and listening. The second section discusses how to navigate professional communication challenges, such as boundaries and biases. The third section provides chapters in which mindfulness principles are applied to challenging clinical situations. The fourth section describes effective approaches with challenging populations. Together, the applications in Sections III and IV give the reader concrete examples of mindfulness in action. The last chapter (Section V) outlines methods of promoting lifelong mindful practice.

Although Chapters 3 through 20 can be read in any order, the first two chapters are foundational. They are the basis for the subsequent chapters in the book. The first chapter looks at the need for, and value of, positive encounters in health care and provides simple examples of how powerful these encounters can be for patients. The second chapter presents the central tenets of mindfulness, providing a blueprint for constructing strong, supportive, and effective patient–provider interactions. This second chapter holds the key concepts around which the rest of the book is oriented. The reader is encouraged to use this chapter as a compendium of mindfulness principles to be returned to frequently while reading subsequent chapters. Periodically reviewing Chapter 2 will help the reader build mastery of subsequent content and serves to reinforce the central ideas and skills.

Several chapters contain case-based examples of patient care situations that highlight the theme of that chapter. These scenarios are constructed from actual patient cases, but important details have been deleted or substantially modified in order to obscure any potentially identifying features. So, although they are based on fact, the scenarios are essentially fictionalized accounts of relatively common patient care situations.

Some of these scenarios describe *effective* clinician behaviors. Other scenarios describe situations in which providers struggled to provide compassionate care. The less effective scenarios are included not to induce reader guilt (most of us will be able to identify ourselves in similar situations) but to demonstrate how easy it is for us to fall into habitual, sometimes problematic, ways of behaving—not because we lack compassion but because our attention is often pulled away from patients' needs. Please read each of these scenarios with a willingness to consider their potential merit in opening up possibilities for more therapeutic interactions with patients and families and, therefore, the opportunity for greater professional satisfaction.

The themes contained within these scenarios and within each of the chapters are multifaceted and at times overlap. Cases presented in one chapter may be relevant to themes presented in a subsequent chapter. For example, in Chapter 1, the reader is introduced to Mark O'Brien, whose struggle with alcoholism is presented as an illustration of the power clinicians have when they seize the opportunity to unfailingly create positive encounters with patients. By extending consistently positive regard toward a patient struggling with substance abuse, the efforts of the clinicians involved proved to be truly transformative. But Mark's story also serves as a depiction of how those same clinicians were able to transcend their own biases in order to allow Mark to see himself differently. This transcendence is described in more detail in Chapter 19, where substance abuse is the central focus.

The scenarios depicted throughout the book involve practitioners primarily from medicine and nursing. Nurses and physicians, trainees, social workers, and others are also presented in examples. However, with slight modifications, the scenarios are applicable across disciplines. Although the roles of nurses, social workers, and physicians certainly vary, the fundamental principles for establishing effective patient–provider encounters remain constant. And although the primary aim of this book is to promote mindfulness as a powerful method of enhancing patient–provider communication, the secondary aim is to promote mindfulness as a means of enhancing cross-disciplinary understanding. To operate compassionately in today's health care systems requires all of us to understand, identify with, and support our colleagues in other disciplines and acknowledge the common struggles we share as we join together in the coordinated care of our patients.

Theresa Raphael-Grimm

Encounters 1

*H*umans thrive on relationships. Positive interactions are the essence of our happiness (Fredrickson, 2013). Often such positive interactions occur in very brief encounters, even with relative strangers, where people share a moment of connectedness. Connecting to others, in a positive way, is affirming. It allows us to feel like we belong to our community, and it decreases our sense of isolation. There is perhaps no more important time for people to feel connected to and supported by others as when they face a serious illness or trauma.

When entering the health care system, patients move through seemingly countless encounters with a wide variety of personnel. The quality of each of those encounters matters. When sick or injured, people are at their most vulnerable. Often worried, embarrassed, and sometimes in fear of death, people navigating the health care system are especially sensitive to the manner in which they are treated. From the clerk at the check-in desk, to the technician manning the EKG machine, to the nurse conducting the initial assessment or the physician completing the history and physical exam, encounters accumulate to create an impression of the relative *goodness* or *badness* of the experience. Even in commonplace encounters, as mundane as providing directions to the cafeteria or guidance about flu shots, clinicians and staff extend small gestures of warmth and goodwill, and seize opportunities for extending support and comfort.

Every encounter provides an opportunity for the patient to experience the healing power of our full attention, to feel valued, cared for, respected, and understood (Ferrucci, 2006). But many times, even well-meaning personnel undermine these opportunities, often through a kind of mindlessness, oblivious to the manner in which they engage in their work. From the clerk preoccupied with forms and signatures, to the physical therapist who provides treatment with a robotic, inflexible demeanor and scripted phrases—such interactions convey a lack of interest in the patient's individual plight and a rote-like attention to products over process. Such approaches often serve to increase, rather than reduce, a patient's suffering. As Daniel Goleman noted: "A prerequisite to empathy is simply paying attention to the person in pain" (Goleman, 2013).

Because it is easy to forget the impact we have, or what it is like to be in a patient's shoes, we can easily minimize these critical moments, reducing them to mere spaces in time for getting the job done. We've all been involved in encounters where we were treated in routine, perfunctory ways, or sometimes even as inconveniences. And yet, most people who pursue careers in the health professions do so with a sincere interest in, and commitment to, contributing to the collective social good, to "making a difference" in the lives of patients and families. So how do such virtuous and well-meaning people evolve into time-pressured, preoccupied, procedure-driven clinicians who appear to be functioning on autopilot?

Through time and acclimation, the culture of the health care system becomes second nature—so familiar as to be rendered invisible to those of us accustomed to functioning within it. With so much of health care being driven by productivity standards, time becomes an ever more precious commodity. Clinicians and staff find themselves inadvertently engaged in a perpetual game of "beat the clock." Getting the job done easily and efficiently can become the primary objective. The *manner* in which that job gets done becomes secondary.

Yet for patients, this same health care culture is a confusing maze of clinics and procedures, instructions and interventions, with unfamiliar personnel sometimes giving conflicting information, all of which serves to make the illness experience very difficult to navigate. For patients, our medical institutions are foreign lands filled with customs, traditions, and expectations that are often confusing, counterintuitive, and disconcerting. They are places where patients are expected to conform to these customs, be ever cooperative and compliant, and submit to unwelcome ministrations no matter how uncomfortable or ill timed. In fact, patients are commonly labeled as "difficult" if they question the value of their care, or if they resist treatments that are expensive, inconvenient, time-consuming, or painful. When they most need the support and positive regard of their caregivers, some patients are met with a kind of prejudice for asking too many questions or for balking at costs or confinements, or simply for taking up too much time. Interactions that strain patient–provider relationships are far more costly for the patient than for the caregiver.

One study suggests that 85% of patients believe that strong relationships, effective communication, and emotional support within health care are very important to successful medical treatment, and 81% believe that such relationships influence whether a patient lives or dies (Lown, Rosen, & Marttila, 2011). Similar perceptions are reported among cancer patients (Thorne, Hislop, Armstrong, & Oglov, 2008). In fact, these patients linked helpful communication with psychological comfort, feelings of hopefulness, and a sense that they were active agents in their own care. Conversely, participants associated unhelpful communication with psychological distress, feeling dehumanized, and feelings of despair (Thorne et al., 2008).

Patients who are perceived to be difficult or demanding are at greater risk for experiencing nontherapeutic encounters. They are often seen less frequently, are seen for shorter lengths of time, and are commonly avoided by care personnel. And although it is true that some patients or family members demonstrate difficult behaviors that providers find challenging, creating effective relationships with such patients is still possible, especially if clinicians depersonalize patients' behaviors and rethink their own expectations. Supporting patients is not necessarily synonymous with clinicians "liking" them. It is possible to extend compassion even to those patients whose behaviors we find taxing or tedious or even rude, if our efforts can remain centered around the goals of both seeking to understand and conveying a desire to help.

Much of establishing effective relationships is about transcending our own judgments or knee-jerk reactions and operating from a place of intentional focus, where understanding the patient's thoughts, feelings, and needs are at the center of our efforts. Such is the popular philosophy of "patient-centered care." In order to provide patient-centered care, clinicians need guidelines for how they can consistently assume the kind of demeanor that makes such care part of a conscious choice, a way of being in the health care world.

4

If professionals can hold to a core principle, one that asserts that in the treatment of each patient there is a need to establish some level of positive regard, then within those relationships, compassion will have a chance to form and empathy to be conveyed. Suchman and Matthews (1988) refer to this as the "connexional dimension" of care where "basic human needs for connection and meaning are met" (Suchman & Matthews, 1988, p. 125), and they emphasize that these connections are central to medical care. Relationships are at the core of all effective health care encounters and serve to enhance the experience for both the patient and the practitioner (Gunderman, 2013).

Within effective relationships lies the power to heal. Trust has the potential to form if the patient believes that the provider is trying to understand, willing to listen, and able to provide care that meets at least some of the patient's needs. These are the essentials of effective relationship building and provide the scaffolding on which interventions are layered.

It has long been understood that manner matters. The arrogant surgeon, the battle-axe nurse, and the flippant orderly are time-worn caricatures well represented in movies and television as sources of disdain, or even humor, but for the vulnerable patient, personnel who demonstrate such traits can be sources of real and unnecessary suffering. In such adversarial relationships, patients experience considerable distress, often with a sense of "being in it alone" without the care, concern, and wisdom of providers from whom they had hoped to draw strength, comfort, and reassurance.

Sometimes relationships simply don't form. Clinicians move through their day with polite, perfunctory banter but without a sense of having shared any kind of bond or authentic interaction. Frederickson (2013) describes these as pseudo-interactions, where the person "goes through the motions" but with little real investment or concern. Although certainly not inflicting trauma, these kinds of encounters can leave the patient feeling cold or disconnected (Fredrickson, 2013).

Much of healing happens in encounters, even brief ones, where two people share a moment of authentic concern and human connection, where the patient experiences a sense that his or her suffering matters to the clinician and that the clinician is joining with the patient in attempting to alleviate that suffering. Such relationships may last only minutes, as in the case of the night nurse who answers a patient's call light and says with sincere interest: "Mr. Miller, you look uncomfortable. What can I do to help?" She recognizes his suffering and allows him an opportunity to convey any concern, physical or emotional, with a willingness to try to address it. He describes agitation, and on further questioning, admits he is terrified to learn the results of his treatment—the verdict is coming with 7 a.m. rounds.

Although words matter, demeanor matters even more. Mindfully, deliberately assuming a posture of willingness, interest, and respect, of wanting to understand, sets the stage for healing encounters to unfold. So often physicians and nurses fall into the trap of believing that their value to patients and families rests primarily with their medical knowledge base and their mastery of cutting-edge treatments, and although these are certainly vital to competent care, more often it is in clinicians' interpersonal skills and their emotional intelligence where their power to heal resides. It is the ability to "cultivate genuinely positive social sentiments from the inside out" that Frederickson (2013, p. 96) cites as the foundation of successful encounters. Feigned concern, forced and insincere, can be as detrimental as no concern at all. Sincerity and earnestness, in the effort to create a healing encounter, are critical to the effort's success. Without sincerity, distrust finds a toehold.

It is not only compassionate but also pragmatic for clinicians to develop effective relationships with patients and families. Patients who believe that their providers are supportive, invested, and empathic are much more satisfied with their care. Even in situations where patients believe that their treatment was inadequate or even harmful, they are less likely to engage in legal action if they also believe that their providers cared about them, acted in good faith, and had their best interests at heart (Levinson, Roter, Mullooly, Dull, & Frankel, 1997).

Joining with patients, as partners in their care, with the goal of achieving the best possible health outcomes, represents a willingness to walk with patients on their illness journey, even if it is only for a few miles of the trip. The power of a positive encounter provides the patient with comfort and the practitioner a sense of meaning and purpose, of having shared in the patient's critical life moments in a way that positively influenced the patient's experience, even during the patient's transition to death.

Positive encounters are good for everyone. The challenge comes in creating them consciously, consistently, and in a time-efficient manner, and doing so even in situations seemingly fraught with interpersonal barriers. This requires mindfulness, a calm, deliberate, and thoughtful effort at observing and transcending one's own inner experience; being able to anticipate the needs, emotions, and thoughts of others; and moving through encounters with awareness and empathic intention, fully present.

The Power of Positive Regard

There is perhaps no other patient population that meets with more clinician negativity than those suffering with substance abuse. The stigma is deep and widespread (more about this in Chapter 19). Compassion, it seems, has its limits, especially toward people who are not "like us" (Wilson, 1998).

Case

Mark O'Brien was a 38-year-old alcoholic when his physician told him that if he didn't stop drinking he would destroy his liver beyond any hope of recovery. Mark had been raised in an Irish American family where beer drinking was part of the culture, and Mark started drinking at an early age, but it wasn't until college that he began drinking heavily. Being an introvert by nature, Mark found it easier, under the influence of alcohol, to socialize at parties and talk to women. Upon graduation, he landed a good job, but found himself habitually consuming at least a six-pack, sometimes two, every night. His girlfriend eventually left him as alcohol began to sabotage everything they'd been working toward: stable jobs, a good relationship, an eye toward marriage and building a family. The alcohol insidiously became more important than the job, the relationship, or the future. Mark was alone, depressed, and guilty. Having come from a stoic culture where males were expected to act with strength, determination, and power, getting help was out of the question. Instead, Mark self-medicated. He drank even more to try to numb himself from the feelings of regret and despair.

With his liver at risk, Mark reluctantly entered a hospital-based detox center. There he encountered nurses and physicians who, from his report, seemed to resent having to care for him. The underlying message was "we have real, sick people to deal with; we don't want to spend our time and effort on some low-life drunk who got himself into this predicament and will likely go right back to drinking after he leaves." Mark felt even more worthless when he left the detox center, having received validation that he truly was a despicable person, not worth anyone's time or attention. The pain of this was overwhelming, and after a few days of physical and mental turmoil, he went back to using the only form of relief that he had readily available: alcohol.

A second, subsequent hospital admission was similar to the first, and again, upon discharge, Mark returned to drinking. Finally, Mark's physical status had deteriorated to such a degree that his primary care provider referred him to a substance abuse specialist who had him admitted to a new inpatient treatment program based on an alternate philosophy of care. There, he experienced a very different atmosphere. Encounters with the staff were uniformly positive. Mark entered the program despite his own strong sense of futility, believing that this experience would mimic those of his prior hospital stays. Instead, he encountered clinicians who deliberately avoided the tendency to form negative judgments while consciously conveying warmth and kindness. They addressed Mark's needs with equanimity and compassion. Schooled in an alternate approach to substance abuse treatment, these clinicians reinforced to him his intrinsic value and his capacity to find meaning and purpose in his life. The dignity and respect with which he was treated represented an enormous departure from what Mark had previously experienced. For the first time in years, Mark began to feel that there was something within him worth saving. He left the unit determined to make a change. He remained sober, returned to college, became a nurse, and devoted his subsequent 25-year professional life to the treatment of people struggling with substance abuse. He attributes his recovery, even his life, to the nurses and physicians who treated him respectfully, with dignity and warmth, in a manner that helped him regain his own self-respect and hope for a meaningful future. The power of positive regard, conveyed to patients through even the shortest of encounters, can be not only life changing but life saving.

References

Ferrucci, P. (2006). *The power of kindness: The unexpected benefits of leading a compassionate life.* New York, NY: J. P. Tarcher/Penguin.

Fredrickson, B. (2013). *Love 2.0: How our supreme emotion affects everything we think, do, feel, and become.* New York, NY: Hudson Street Press.

Goleman, D. (2013). *Curing the common cold of leadership: Poor listening.* Retrieved January 24, 2014, from http://www.linkedin.com/today/post/article/20130502140433-117825785-curing-the-common-cold-of-leadership-poor-listening

Gunderman, R. B. (2013). A prescription for what ails medical education. *Chronicle of Higher Education, 60*(16), A60.

Levinson, W., Roter, D. L., Mullooly, J. P., Dull, V. T., & Frankel, R. M. (1997). Physician–patient communication. The relationship with malpractice claims among primary care physicians and surgeons. *The Journal of the American Medical Association, 277*(7), 553–559.

Lown, B. A., Rosen, J., & Marttila, J. (2011). An agenda for improving compassionate care: A survey shows about half of patients say such care is missing. *Health Affairs, 30*(9), 1772–1778. doi: 10.1377/hlthaff.2011.0539

Suchman, A. L., & Matthews, D. A. (1988). What makes the patient–doctor relationship therapeutic? Exploring the connexional dimension of medical care. *Annals of Internal Medicine, 108*(1), 125–130.

Thorne, S. E., Hislop, T. G., Armstrong, E. A., & Oglov, V. (2008). Cancer care communication: The power to harm and the power to heal? *Patient Education and Counseling, 71*(1), 34–40. doi: 10.1016/j.pec.2007.11.010

Wilson, E. O. (1998, April). Biological basis of morality: Do we invent our moral absolutes in order to make society workable? *The Atlantic, 281*, 53–54, 56+.

Mindfulness 2

Mindfulness Described

Mindfulness is a state of awareness, or consciousness, that is fostered by the consistent and deliberate effort to take notice of what is occurring in one's inner and outer worlds, with a capacity to be fully engaged in the present moment, rather than distracted by, preoccupied with, or focused on the past or future. To be mindful is to be attuned to one's internal climate and with that awareness, make more conscious decisions about how to respond to everyday events in the "here and now." It enhances the capacity to take notice of the subtle shifts in our emotions and thoughts and consider how those emotions and thoughts might influence our attitudes and drive our behaviors (Brown, Ryan, & Creswell, 2007).

Mindfulness practice hones our ability to notice those internal changes that occur when events or experiences cause us discomfort, excitement, pleasure, or pain. Mindfulness skills can provide a kind of rubric to follow in order to avoid reacting unconsciously, habitually, or impulsively because it is from our reactive, impulsive, habitual responses that we find ourselves suffering from a cascade of unintended consequences. These consequences often block us from reaching our intended objective and, at times, can inadvertently cause additional, unnecessary distress. Mindfulness keeps us alert to our internal climate changes; prompts us to consider their origin, meaning, and impact; and helps us to choose wisely from a behavioral repertoire that enables us to act deliberately (rather than reflexively) in a manner that is consistent with our values and goals.

When mindfulness shifts from an internal focus (ourselves) to an external focus (others), it fosters a capacity for openness that allows us to be more sensitive to others and to monitor how our own behavior is impacting them. It fosters a curiosity and a drive to understand the lived experience of others, of the people we encounter in our personal and professional lives, and to offer thoughtful responses that meet the unique demands of those interpersonal situations.

Mindfulness and Health Care

In health care, mindfulness can cultivate within us a desire to know and understand the thoughts, feelings, and needs of patients and their families. With focus shifted outward, to the needs and feelings of others, comes the capacity to be fully present. This presence is a critical element in helping patients heal (Siegel, 2010a). In other words, mindfulness helps us to self-monitor so that we can respond effectively to meet the needs of the patients and families.

Mindfulness and Information Processing

Stimuli bombard us every day, sometimes at an unrelenting pace, and examining all of these stimuli all the time requires considerable mental energy. In an effort to decrease the overload, we develop certain processing shortcuts that allow us to move quickly through the demands of the day and categorize, anticipate, and quickly respond to our experiences. Sometimes, use of these automatic-processing shortcuts can result in more simplistic or primitive methods of handling complex interpersonal events. Joshua Greene (2013) offers the camera metaphor to describe this phenomenon. When a camera is set on the automatic function, little is required of the operator. The camera automatically accounts for light, distance, focus, and contrast, in a way that allows the operator to do little more than point and shoot. But in the manual mode, the camera operator consciously chooses the settings in order to create a deliberate effect: allow more light, capture fast action, focus on a specific feature, and so forth. In the case of a medical emergency, personnel need to function in automatic mode, in well-practiced ways, carrying out quick and highly specialized functions in order to urgently save a life. But with the usual types of interpersonal interactions, typical of common health care encounters, more deliberate, reflective, and thoughtful action is required. In these situations clinicians need to be in "manual" mode. We need to carefully, thoughtfully consider that the quality of the interpersonal interaction is as important as the more concrete tasks of patient assessment, interviewing, health teaching, lifestyle advising, and other concerns. The manner in which we engage patients needs to be deliberate, with proper, intentional adjustments made to the ways in which we use ourselves as therapeutic tools. More objective, creative, and deliberate methods of analyzing and evaluating input with a willingness to examine things from multiple perspectives are key elements of critical thinking (Paul & Elder, 2009). Without reflection and conscious consideration, our responses can become habitual, and sometimes even harmful. To reiterate: Knee-jerk reactions are effective when we need to act quickly in situations of urgency, but in most of our professional communication, where we are deliberately engaged in creating important and meaningful interactions, paying more conscious attention to the nuances of our own behaviors and the subtlety of patient needs is required (Siegel, 2010a).

Such attention means that we have to carry a kind of dual awareness: a capacity to monitor ourselves while assessing the impact that our behaviors are having on others. It requires us to be keenly attuned to "me and you" almost simultaneously (Gerlach, 2013). Gerlach describes this dual awareness as a process where one person—in this case, the health care provider (HCP)—is aware of, and seeks to understand, the thoughts, feelings, and needs of the patient while paying attention to the thoughts, feelings, and needs within him- or herself. With this dual awareness in place, the HCP is much better able to examine, step back, and observe the communication process as it unfolds, to detect when problems arise, and to seek clarification and apply correction before the process deteriorates into something that becomes nontherapeutic.

Stated another way: Mindfulness allows us to conduct the ongoing assessments required for the "therapeutic use of self." We monitor the manner in which we are conducting ourselves but also the responses that we are eliciting from others. As partners in a type of communication dance, we stay attuned to our own shifting thoughts, feelings, and needs, conscious of how these might influence our behaviors. Then, with this attunement in place, we choose actions that will best serve our care goals. At the same time, we remain sensitive to the thoughts, feelings, and needs of patients and families. We provide an atmosphere of acceptance and openness that allows their fears, sorrows, concerns, and questions to be expressed.

Clinical Example

Clinton Jennings is a nurse practitioner who works in the outpatient oncology clinic of a large, university medical center. He has a long, tedious drive to work, and sometimes, like this morning, his commute is made worse by a major traffic tie-up. Having stayed up late last night, listening to his wife describe her distress at his long work hours and almost constant fatigue, he starts the day feeling especially frustrated, angry, and entitled. He is driving aggressively, making sure to cut off any motorists who attempt to merge in ahead of him. When he arrives at the hospital, before heading to the clinic, he stops off at the coffee kiosk. The line is long, the service is slow, and after 10 minutes of agitated waiting, he leaves, his need for caffeine unfulfilled. As he walks into the clinic, Angela, the clinic secretary, greets him with a cheerful "Good morning, Clint." He responds angrily with "What's so good about it?" His first patient, Maurice Jones, overhears this interchange from the waiting room. Mr. Jones has returned to the clinic to undergo a workup for possible recurrence of his lung cancer. He had planned to use his appointment to ask Clint several questions about his prognosis and share some fears that have been on his mind. Having witnessed Clint's demeanor, Mr. Jones decides to keep his worries to himself. He has been feeling so emotionally fragile that he's afraid he will become tearful if Clint meets his questions with an angry or frustrated demeanor. With his decision to remain silent,

Mr. Jones experiences a sense of disappointment, sadness, and isolation. In other words, his suffering grows.

This example demonstrates that even when a clinician's behavior is *not* directed toward the patient—in fact, Clint was not even paying attention to whether his demeanor could be witnessed by anyone other than the secretary—it still can have a profound effect. The vulnerability that patients feel is unlike any other. Although interventions such as addressing patients' questions and providing support and reassurance are routine for Clint, this is foreign territory for Mr. Jones, who has no idea how Clint usually responds to patient concerns. Mr. Jones has never before had to deeply consider his own mortality, or experience the many worries that surface when facing terminal illness. Much of Mr. Jones's suffering could have been mitigated through a warm, positive, and accepting encounter with Clint. But today, that opportunity has been lost.

If he had been able to operate from mindfulness, Clint might have been able to start his day aware of his own stressors, identify his emotions, consider effective strategies, move into the present moment, and imagine how his agitated state might predispose him to acting insensitively. Having identified the details of his internal distress, he could then potentially regain his equilibrium; resume a calm, open, and compassionate countenance; and be in a better position to mitigate the suffering of his patients. Operating from a place of mindfulness, Clinton might have used his morning drive to think through the validity of his wife's perspective, deliberately engage in calming exercises and considering what he could do to improve the situation. He could make a plan of action for how to adjust his mindset in order to get through the day effectively. When he returned home, he could have more calmly, sensitively, and less defensively addressed his wife's concerns. Traffic jams are rarely a welcome experience, but this morning Clint could have used the extra time to deliberately work to regulate his emotions. He could focus his attention, examine his work situation, identify those aspects of his job that are amenable to change, consider alternatives, and decide on a plan of action. Traffic *is* frustrating, but with the skillful practice of mindfulness it can be endured (occasionally even welcomed) and considered as a time to step back and observe thoughts and emotions, and thereby avoid potentially reactive, and often ineffective, responses.

Mindful Identification and Self-Correction

Taking on the posture of an observer of our own internal climate allows for identification of emotions, issues, and concerns. As a mindful observer of his own lived experience, Clint can consciously explore his inner experience and observe and describe what he discovers. In doing so, his internal dialog is likely to go something like this: "I hate it when the traffic gets tied up and I'm already running late. I'm tired, tense, and frustrated." In this statement it is evident that as he takes a step back and becomes an observer of his own inner climate, he has included a scan of his body to assess his physical state, (what Moorhead refers to as entering "Body Mind"; personal communication, January 22, 2014). Clint notes that he is both tired and tense. He then directs his internal observations toward his emotional state, to a metaphorical place that some refer to as "Emotional Mind" (Linehan, 1993b). In doing so, Clint finds that he is angry and frustrated. When he deliberately shifts to examining the situation logically by considering just the facts of the situation, he is in "Reasonable Mind" (Linehan, 1993b), and his internal dialog sounds something like: "People get emotional when they are tired. I am driving aggressively." Using the data about his thoughts, emotions, and physical sensations, he draws some conclusions. Synthesizing and summarizing the data are considered to be an exercise in wisdom or "Wise Mind" (Linehan, 1993b). In Wise Mind, Clint's internal dialog takes on a different tone and is reflected in the following words: "Getting worked up won't be very effective in successfully getting through my day. These thoughts are only making me feel worse. I need to bring my calmest self to the clinic so that I can be fully present and attend to the patients." He then deliberately chooses to engage in a set of skills that he knows will help him become centered and better able to meet current demands. Now his inner voice is saying: "Let me take a few deep breaths and use this time in the car to think through my wife's concerns, strategize, and calm down."

Personal stress, time pressure, a full schedule, vulnerable patients—these are common features of a health care professional's life. Adopting a deliberate posture of mindfulness allows the savvy clinician to notice the mounting frustration growing within him or her, and take a momentary "time out" to consider what patients need, how vulnerable patients often feel, and how powerful an effective encounter can be. The clinician can re-think the meaning and value of his or her role, and the value of entering a state of internal calm before interacting with patients and families. The clinician can rebalance his or her internal emotional equilibrium so as to be ready to then focus attention outward on the thoughts, feelings, and needs of patients. Mindfulness allows the clinician to deliberately assume a more accepting posture and a more purposeful state of mind.

Domains of Mindfulness

Marsha Linehan (1993a) describes mindfulness as a core skill. Although her work targets mindfulness as a central principle within a specific type of psychotherapy, philosophers, researchers, and followers of Eastern spiritual practices have identified the value of mindfulness as a primary means of increasing general well-being. In fact, multiple studies now support the use of mindfulness as a central coping strategy in dealing with all manner of stress, preventing burnout, and enhancing empathy among health care professionals (Krasner et al., 2009). Mindfulness-based stress-reduction programs are now widely available and are found to decrease suffering and enhance well-being in both patients and clinicians alike. Mindfulness practice is thought to promote people's awareness of, and conscious responses to, their internal climate so as to decrease work stress, enhance compassion, mitigate burnout, increase empathy (Brown & Ryan, 2003), and improve emotion regulation (Teper, Segal, & Inzlicht, 2013).

Building on the work of Linehan (1993b) and M. Moorhead (personal communication, January 22, 2014), and with content review by C. Forneris (personal communication, January 10, 2014), this book uses a hybrid States of Mind framework for conceptualizing our internal climate. This hybrid model is reflected in the Venn diagram shown in Figure 2.1 and is meant to illustrate the four distinct but overlapping domains of inner experience, or states of mind. For simplicity, these domains are referred to here as Emotion Mind, Reason Mind, Body Mind, and Wise Mind, with Wise Mind representing the synthesis of the other three, where mind states converge and from which more effective and deliberate behavioral responses are thought to emerge.

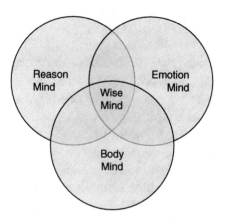

FIGURE 2.1 Hybrid version of States of Mind framework.

Source: Moorhead (personal communication).

This rendering of the States of Mind framework is meant to give the reader a concrete conceptualization of the domains of experience that influence our thoughts and behaviors. Because these influences are often outside of our immediate awareness, the States of Mind framework helps us to think concretely about each domain and identify from what part of our inner experience our thoughts, attitudes, assumptions, and reactions may be originating. It is understood that the diagram represents a simplistic illustration of a complex process, and is not meant as a literal depiction of neuroanatomy or physiology.

Emotion Mind can be thought of as the domain where emotional thinking dominates; this dominance is often evident when our internal dialogs begin to sound something like the following: "I hate this situation. Why should I have to put up with this? I don't deserve to be treated this way!" But it also surfaces in the face of satisfying emotions: "I did a great patient presentation in rounds this morning and was really on my game." Whether the emotions are positive or negative, pleasant or unpleasant, they play a critical role in informing us about the nature of our experience. Emotions often exert a powerful force on our desire to replicate, or avoid, the circumstances around which the emotions occur. This is why we are often drawn to repeat behaviors that have resulted in pleasure and avoid situations that cause emotional pain. Acting solely from Emotion Mind is problematic when emotions take over, driving our behaviors in situations when more thoughtful, reasoned, and deliberate consideration is important and when circumstances call for a controlled behavioral response. Emotions can cause us to act impulsively, or with habitual reactivity that can ultimately undermine our effectiveness.

Body Mind is the awareness of our physical experiences, the way in which the body is responding to stimuli: "My stomach is in knots, my teeth are clenched, and my body is so tense that it hurts." Or, "I'm tired, hungry, and haven't had a chance to go to the bathroom for 2 hours." Or, "I feel satisfied when I hit the vein on the first stick." Or even, "This bath feels so luxurious, and soothing." By scanning our bodies for data, we sometimes detect important indicators that we are more emotionally activated than we realize or that a physical discomfort is interfering with our ability to focus. And these data can be very useful in prompting us to address our needs and to calm ourselves before acting on our experiences.

Reason Mind is the metaphorical place where more analytical, more measured, controlled thoughts enter our consciousness: "I know that people with cancer have worries that they need to express." "People who have poor prognoses often have lots of concerns and it is important to address those concerns, even if it takes extra time in clinic." "I know I tend to be irritable when I've not had enough sleep." Or "I know my stomach gets into knots when I have to deal with an angry patient. I need to mentally review the conflict resolution skills before I approach the angry patient."

Wise Mind is a conceptual construct defined as the area of overlap between the other three domains. It is a place of discernment where motives, biases, and intuitions that had been identified in other domains are purposely examined, and self-regulatory efforts are imposed. Wise Mind houses the kind of analytic processes that Croskerry (2013) identifies as metacognition, wherein we think about our thinking and clearly monitor which motives, desires, and biases are at play, paying careful attention to how those motives, desires, and biases might corrupt our judgment.

In Wise Mind the internal dialog may sound something like this: "I don't like this situation and I don't like having to deal with my wife's complaints, but that doesn't mean that I cannot cope with it. I have the capacity to function effectively, and if I calm down and stop reacting, I will feel better and hopefully be able to provide some comfort to the patients I will see today in the clinic. I understand my wife's perspective, and sometimes feel helpless in being able to do anything about her concerns, and my tension in these situations is often felt in my body. Rather than fight with her, I need to try to see it her way and begin to consider some solutions. In the meantime, I need to refocus my attention on my patients and try to respond to them with warmth and compassion. Doing so always helps me feel better."

Domains of Mind in Action

Emotions are important informants of our internal state. They influence us in an intuitive way and provide much of our life's joy and depth. Emotions of love, sympathy, fear, anger, embarrassment, and frustration provide data about the nature of any given situation. Problems arise when emotions become so dominant in our experience that they *drive* rather than *inform* behavior. The cute puppy in the pet store window tugs at our heartstrings, fills us with excitement and longing (Emotion Mind), meets our physical need for contact and warmth (Body Mind), and moves us to want to take him home. But a year later when his 95-pound body seems to overwhelm a small apartment and his constant barking at loud neighbors has the landlord issuing warnings for noise violations, feelings of frustration and regret are likely to emerge, with thoughts of "How could I have been so shortsighted?" Emotions need to be detected, examined, and respected but often require the scrutiny of Reason Mind to be kept in check. But use of Reason Mind alone can be equally as problematic. Getting a pet hamster, instead of a dog, because it is practical, containable, and quiet may make logistical sense, but may not provide the sense of warmth, comfort, or companionship that is so much a part of owning a pet. It makes sense, but it doesn't meet the important emotional and physical needs that prompted the desire for a dog in the first place. By assuming a Wise Mind posture, we become more able to weigh the pros and cons and look at ideas for compromise. Wise Mind acknowledges the value of meeting emotional needs while not allowing emotions alone to dominate decision making or behavior. A Wise Mind compromise in the pet situation just described might be to consider the ownership of a cat—a cat is small and quiet but able to meet the owner's emotional and physical needs in its capacity to be affectionate and comforting, and a year later, leave its owner content and satisfied.

Health Care Example

Emotion Mind thinking is evident in the case of Jamal Jones. Jamal is a third-year medical student doing his first surgery rotation. He has been assigned by the surgery resident to meet with Mr. Adams, a patient about to undergo an emergency appendectomy. Jamal has been instructed to explain to Mr. Adams the nature of the surgery so that the resident can soon stop by and quickly request Mr. Adams to sign the consent form. Jamal is feeling uncertain about this assignment. He knows about the basics of appendectomies but he doesn't know much about the details, but he wants to impress his resident and Mr. Adams with his sophisticated knowledge of anatomy. He introduces himself to the patient and launches into a long description of abdominal anatomy and the relative value of abdominal organs when Mr. Adams asks, "What do you mean when you say that I don't need my appendix? If God gave me an appendix, I must need it!" Jamal is feeling frustrated. His resident is likely to come into the room at any moment, consent form in hand, expecting that Jamal has done a thorough job preparing the patient. Jamal realizes that the patient is not responding well to his approach, but doesn't take the time to try to consider the patient's thoughts, feelings, and needs. Jamal is preoccupied with wanting to look competent, even a little important, and in a manner that will make Jamal look good to his supervisor. Jamal, feeling his jaw tense and his hands get sweaty, says "Look, Mr. Adams, just take my word for it, you don't need your appendix. It's just an evolutionary remnant. You'll be better off without it." Mr. Adams cuts him off: "Are you saying that you know better than God about whether my appendix is needed and that I'm supposed to trust the opinion of a medical student?" Jamal is now insulted; he rolls his

eyes and wears a disgusted facial expression as he is thinking how annoying it is to try to explain things to a simple-minded laborer. While Jamal is mentally denigrating
Mr. Adams, Jeff, the chief surgery resident, enters the room.
Anxious and annoyed, Jamal tells Jeff that it seems as if
Mr. Adams doesn't really want to get treatment for his pain
and believes that the surgeons don't know what they are
doing. Mr. Adams, now visibly angry, tells Jeff that Jamal is
an arrogant idiot and demands that Jamal leave the room.

Using a more mindful approach, Jamal might have anticipated that Mr. Adams, a laborer with a strong Christian
belief system who has never been hospitalized before,
may have a limited knowledge of, or interest in, complex
medical details. Because Mr. Adams is experiencing intense
abdominal pain and fever, his most immediate need is for
pain relief. Given his physical discomfort, he is likely to be
irritable and to have limited tolerance for long explanations filled with jargon. Likely Mr. Adams needs to sense
that whoever comes into his room will have some sensitivity for his suffering. Mr. Adams wants to be heard, understood, and valued. He wants someone to validate that his
condition is painful and explain, simply, how the team will
address it. Mr. Adams wants to know that his care is being
planned carefully and managed efficiently, and that any
procedures will be explained to him clearly, briefly, and
with an eye toward respecting his religious beliefs. Many
of this patient's needs could have been anticipated by Jamal
if Jamal had taken a minute to think through the patient's
likely thoughts, feelings, and needs and used this as a base
from which to operate. Then, before meeting the patient,
Jamal could have scanned his own inner climate. He could
tap into his own emotions, motives, and desires. He could
identify his body's tension, a tension that is accompanied
by a sense of urgency. He could acknowledge that these

internal factors could influence his behavior as he reasons through how to balance his own concerns with the needs and concerns of the patient.

From the patient's perspective, clinician competence is less about demonstrating deep knowledge of anatomy and physiology and more about expressing compassion and translating medical information in a manner that provides the best possible level of understanding. Although Jamal is understandably proud of his academic accomplishments, and has been socialized into a role where demonstrating his subject mastery is a habitual form of exhibiting competence, he needs to be able to shift focus. The patient is not his audience. Rather, it is the patient who is the focus of clinical attention. This fact appears, on the surface, to be obvious, but clinicians' need for recognition, positive regard, and elevated status frequently interfere with effective inter-personal interaction. With mindfulness, clinicians have an opportunity to examine their internal "equipment," examine the care machinery for "bugs," and recalibrate the mechanisms in order to shift back to *patient-centered* care.

Being aware of, and able to identify, the emotions we are experiencing are the first steps to recalibration. Is anxiety responsible for Jamal using his expertise in anatomy and physiology as a screen for hiding his discomfort with describing the appendectomy procedure? Is he fearful of looking stupid to the patient, and then failing in his task, making him appear incompetent to the surgery resident? Having made the initial missteps, is he then feeling frustrated at having to deal with an angry patient, and if unaware of that frustration, is he more likely to respond to the patient in an angry and impatient manner?

But, if he is aware of his feelings, he has the opportunity to acknowledge them, and then use reason to think through alternate methods of addressing the situation. If he were able to identify his anxiety from the beginning, he could then acknowledge it. If he were able to acknowledge that his anxiety was fueling a desire to hide behind his knowledge of anatomy, he could then select another course of action. He could move into Reason Mind and determine that course of action by considering that if his goal is to help the patient better understand his treatment, then he likely needs to think about who this patient is—about the patient's potential thoughts, feelings, and needs—and to plan his strategy accordingly. With such an approach, he might have been able to avoid eliciting the patient's anger. Listening to, validating, and accepting the patient's perspectives, rather than reacting defensively, would better serve his goals.

The Mindfulness Process

First, look inward:

Focus on one state of mind at a time.

Assess *emotional* temperature (Emotion Mind):
> What emotions am I experiencing? (Name each one; e.g., anger, resentment, anxiety, disgust, sadness, etc.)
> How intense are these emotions?
> How are my emotions being expressed in my internal dialog?
>> Example: "This stinks. I've got to hurry up. Can't he see I'm busy?"

Assess *physical* sensations (Body Mind):
> Am I tired, hungry, or in pain?
> Am I irritable or agitated, or feeling rushed?

Is my pulse increased; am I perspiring?

Is my stomach in knots, my jaw tense, my face tight?

What is my facial expression?

Does my head feel full, under pressure, or like it's going to explode?

Assess capacity for *reason* and tap into it (Reason Mind):

Can I think clearly and objectively? Or, am I scattered and preoccupied?

What do I need to consider in order to shift my focus back to the patient?

What ideas, principles, or facts can I draw from that would inform this situation? (Note: With Reason Mind, we can begin to look outward to gather information about others.)

What information do I have about the patient and family?

What are the likely thoughts, feelings, and needs of the patient and family?

What questions do I need to ask the patient that would help inform my strategy?

Deliberately enter a place of *wisdom* (Wise Mind):

How might my emotions interfere with my patient care?

How much of my reactivity is coming from biases or faulty assumptions?

How can I challenge these biases and assumptions?

What do I need to do to self-regulate, calm down, and meet my own basic needs (e.g., deep breathe, eat, focus, do one thing at a time, etc.)?

Given my current logical, physical, and emotional states of mind, what makes sense for me to do first?

How do I need to operate in this situation in order to achieve the most effective outcome?

If I were in the patient's situation, what might I need from my health care providers?

Mindfulness can be enhanced by using skills or tools that:

a. Help to guide the assessment process just described, and
b. Address some of the issues discovered through that process.

Some of these skills were alluded to earlier but warrant more explicit description. These skills reflect the work of M. Linehan (1993a, 1993b):

1. *Be an Objective Observer:* Take a deliberate stance as an objective observer. Turning inward and assessing one's internal state is fostered by being able to look at our inner climate from the perspective of an outsider. We can step back and become an observer of our own thoughts, feelings, and sensations while listening to our internal dialog.
2. *Breathe Deep:* Take a deep breath to interrupt any "fight-or-flight" activation that may already be under way. This imposes a calmer state and reduces anxiety while increasing our ability to take a step back and observe.
3. *Observe and Describe:* Observe and describe what is happening internally, without judgment (Linehan, 1993b). By avoiding criticism or self-condemnation, we can explore the inner landscape more freely, without fear of what we might find. With our defenses down, more becomes visible to our mind's eye.
4. *Participating Fully, in the Present Moment:* Once our inner climate has been examined and we've had a chance to recalibrate and reach inner calm, then we can effectively refocus our attention outward again. With that outward focus in place, we participate in meeting the patient's needs—right here, right now, in the present moment.

5. *Participating One-Mindfully:* This is the deliberate practice of doing one thing at a time, sometimes slowly, sometimes with considerable speed, but focusing our attention first on one thing, then the next.

6. *Distress Tolerance:* Sometimes the emotions we uncover in our inner experience will be distressing. We might uncover feelings of self-doubt or shame or fear. In mindfulness these emotions are considered an inevitable part of life, not feelings to flee from but, rather, feelings that will surface, that are part of being human, and that we all have the capacity to acknowledge and just "sit with."

7. *Acceptance:* This is the notion that sometimes things just are what they are—not what we want or deserve, or not what is fair or just. To accept is not the same as condoning. To accept does not mean that we won't try to work constructively to change the situation. Acceptance is more the idea that "Right here, right now, this is what I'm faced with, and I need to effectively operate within this situation, as it is, rather than get lost in my anger about it or in destructive efforts to immediately make it different." The acceptance process has the flavor of "I don't like this but I can cope with it; it doesn't have to completely disrupt my internal equilibrium."

Skill Application

(Note that some of the skills that are described here have been underlined in order to highlight their use.) Going back to our earlier example of Clint Jennings: For Clint to enter into a more mindful perspective, he had to take a deep breath, step back, and become an observer of his own state. He had to notice that he was feeling stressed and that he was behaving ineffectively (angrily, aggressively), and needed to tune into what he was experiencing both in his thoughts and in his senses.

After deliberately observing his inner state, Clint could then <u>describe</u> to himself what this experience was like. He could identify specific thoughts, emotions, and body sensations that were influencing his experience. He was able to assign words to the experience and use this information to inform his actions. In the corrective scenario, he was able to move through the "<u>observe-and-describe</u>" process <u>without assigning judgment</u>. Clint's mindfulness exercise was not hampered by a judgmental description, such as "You fool, there you go again getting angry and acting like a raging nut on the highway!" but instead with something like the following: "I just cut that guy off when he was trying to merge. My driving gets more aggressive when I'm stressed and angry. I need to slow down. It's not like me to drive aggressively. I need to let people merge into my lane, even if some part of me doesn't like it right now." The nonjudgmental version is less emotional and allows Clint to move into a more effective behavioral response in a more timely fashion. He doesn't get caught up in the self-condemning judgments that often serve only to further inflame anger and fuel discontent.

Having effectively moved through the process of observing and describing without judgment, a person is then free to enter into the current situation, participate <u>one-mindfully, fully present</u>, with focus and attention, in order to more effectively meet the demands of that situation. This seems simple yet can be challenging, especially in situations that are stressful, anxiety producing, or characterized by time urgency. In health care, challenging situations are the nature of the work. Being able to observe, describe, and participate fully means having to do this while also engaging in the dual awareness discussed earlier in this chapter. So many of the tasks of health care require active engagement with patients and families. While using mindfulness to monitor and step back from our own thoughts, feelings, and needs, we need to be simultaneously aware of the likely thoughts, feelings, and needs of others. This dual awareness requires effort, at least at first, because, like any skill, it takes time, energy, motivation, and practice to master.

Again, it is important to remember that mindfulness skills are applied both internally, to assess our own inner climate, and externally, to conduct a more objective appraisal of the situation and chart the most effective course of action. Just as assessing our internal climate requires a nonjudgmental approach, this same nonjudgmental stance is critical to examining our external *situations*. The goal here is to pay attention to our habitual tendency to focus on the good or bad aspects of something (the right or wrong of it, the fair or unfair nature of it), and then to deliberately shift into a mental pattern of just describing it objectively—just the facts. Acknowledging that you don't like it, or that it may be harmful, or that it needs immediate attention, or that it is detrimental is a important part of assessing situations in health care, but this is different from assigning judgments like good or bad, right or wrong. Instead of judging a patient who smokes cigarettes (and now exhibits beginning symptoms of emphysema) as being weak, disgusting, or having a stench, simply see that patient as being addicted to nicotine and in need of smoking-cessation efforts. By deliberately <u>accepting the situation</u>, without getting caught up in how it could or should have been different, we avoid judgmental attitudes and are better able to move into a space of working with the situation as it is.

Smoking cigarettes is detrimental to the client, but that is another issue for another time. Right here, right now, this patient needs treatment, support, and access to effective tools to fight the addiction. The patient does not need condemnation.

Participating "<u>one-mindfully</u>" requires that we be focused on one thing at a time, <u>here and now,</u> in a manner that is <u>fully attentive</u> to the person or activity in front of us. Although multitasking is a hallmark of modern health care and it is critical that all of us move efficiently through the myriad tasks that fill a typical day, in actuality, humans can only do one thing at time. Some activities can be done quickly whereas others cannot, but to do something one-mindfully means giving it our full attention, even for a second, before moving on to the next task.

Example: Electronic Medical Record Systems

Even the most skilled clinician cannot complete fields on a computer screen and simultaneously carry on a meaningful assessment of a patient unless the individual is, in reality, moving from screen to patient rapidly, but with focus, each time he or she makes the shift. It is better for the clinician to state to the patient: "Mrs. Morgan, I need to look at this computer screen to fill out some basic information about your current status and any changes you may be experiencing in your health. When I'm done with this segment of your appointment, I will stop working with the computer and give you my full attention so that we can discuss your concerns and questions." In this way, the patient understands that she will not be competing with the computer for the clinician's attention and will have her concerns addressed later in the appointment. This ability to attend to one thing at a time allows the clinician to efficiently move through the required documentation aspects of the visit (the clinician's own work-mandated job needs) while effectively addressing the needs of the patient. This reflects not only the clinician's commitment to doing one thing at a time, but also a dual awareness of both the clinician's own and the patient's needs.

Distress Tolerance

Distress tolerance is the skill that every clinician can apply when health care situations impose strong Emotion Mind activation, especially in situations where we need to continue to operate effectively at work. Distress tolerance has a dimension of acceptance within it. When we witness the dying breaths of a favorite patient, the outrage of a patient who has experienced a serious complication, or the distress of parents who are experiencing their child's fight for survival, strong emotions are activated; all we can do in that moment is to make a deliberate effort to tolerate those emotions. This includes the effort to see them, name them, and accept that they are natural, valid, and important, and acknowledge that we cannot fully process them now, but that we can cope with the distress we feel, that we have the capacity to bear those emotions and the wherewithal to keep them at bay at least while we need to provide patients and families with care. This nonjudgmental, nonemotional posture can be difficult to assume, especially given the workplace demands and competing priorities that make modern health care environments so stressful, and yet it is just these kinds of mindful efforts that can decrease some of the stress that clinicians commonly experience.

In Summary

Using mindfulness to think about our thinking is a skill that requires consistent and committed practice. It requires a willingness to look inward and a daily decision to do so, to move through the mindfulness process deliberately, intentionally, and with the goal of calming our inner climate so as to bring our best possible selves to the external experiences we face. These skills are part of what Siegel describes in his book *Mindsight* (2010b).

Review: Helpful Hints in the Practice of Mindfulness

1. Embrace the idea that mindfulness matters: Being able to step back, observe our own internal condition, describe it in words, and respond consciously to that condition is a valuable practice that confers considerable advantages in allowing us to act effectively in our life roles.
2. Observe and describe, without judgment: Assigning negative judgments to experiences keeps us tangled up in Emotion Mind, where our ideas can get bogged down in efforts to condemn or defend our thoughts and actions, which can result in impulsive, knee-jerk reactions that interfere with effective living.
3. Mindfulness is enhanced through meditation: Meditation is the practice of bringing your awareness back to the here and now, usually through focusing on your breathing. While hours of meditation are endorsed by some practitioners, others are convinced that even a minute or two of escorting our attention back to our breathing can help us focus, help us feel grounded and

calm, and allow us the mental space to address what we have before us, in the here and now.

4. Observe the "shoulds": Sometimes we can get caught up in thinking about what we believe "should" be happening in this situation, but isn't. We react to situations that are difficult, stressful, tedious, and boring, but the suffering seems to worsen when we believe that the circumstance *should* be different. Emotions are then activated: feeling outraged, or entitled, or superior, or victimized. Sometimes aggressive, insensitive, elitist behaviors follow: "I shouldn't have to wait for this patient to ask these questions. He should have asked me in the beginning of the appointment. Now I have to go and see the next patient and he's wasting my time with these simple-minded concerns. I don't need to be answering these questions; the nurse (or nurse's aide, clerk, intern, etc.) should do it."

5. Think of outcomes first: What outcome do we want to ultimately come from our efforts? With the outcome clearly in mind, it is easier to identify the steps needed to reach it and consider the potential effectiveness of each of the steps.

References

Brown, K. W., & Ryan, R. M. (2003). The benefits of being present: Mindfulness and its role in psychological well-being. *Journal of Personality and Social Psychology, 84*(4), 822–848. doi: 10.1037/0022-3514.84.4.822

Brown, K. W., Ryan, R. M., & Creswell, J. D. (2007). Mindfulness: Theoretical foundations and evidence for its salutary effects. *Psychological Inquiry, 18*(4), 211–237.

Croskerry, P. (2013). From mindless to mindful practice—cognitive bias and clinical decision making. *New England Journal of Medicine, 368*(26), 2445–2448. doi: 10.1056/Nejmp1303712

Gerlach, P. (2013). *Lesson 2 of 7: Learn to communicate effectively.* Retrieved January 24, 2014, from http://sfhelp.org/cx/guide2.htm

Greene, J. D. (2013). *Moral tribes: Emotion, reason, and the gap between us and them.* New York, NY: Penguin Press.

Krasner, M. S., Epstein, R. M., Beckman, H., Suchman, A. L., Chapman, B., Mooney, C. J., & Quill, T. E. (2009). Association of an educational program in mindful communication with burnout, empathy, and attitudes among primary care physicians. *The Journal of the American Medical Association, 302*(12), 1284–1293. doi: 10.1001/jama.2009.1384

Linehan, M. (1993a). *Cognitive behavioral treatment of borderline personality disorder.* New York, NY: Guilford Press.

Linehan, M. (1993b). *Skills training manual for treating borderline personality disorder.* New York, NY: Guilford Press.

Paul, R., & Elder, L. (2009). *Critical thinking: Concepts and tools.* Tomales, CA: Foundation for Critical Thinking.

Siegel, D. J. (2010a). *The mindful therapist: A clinician's guide to mindsight and neural integration* (1st ed.). New York, NY: W. W. Norton & Co.

Siegel, D. J. (2010b). *Mindsight: The new science of personal transformation.* New York, NY: Random House.

Teper, R., Segal, Z. V., & Inzlicht, M. (2013). Inside the Mindful Mind: How mindfulness enhances emotion regulation through improvements in executive control. *Current Directions in Psychological Science, 22*(6), 449–454. doi: 10.1177/0963721413495869

Empathy   3

Importance of Empathy in Patient Care

In every helping profession—nursing, medicine, social work, clinical psychology, and others—empathy is considered a fundamental characteristic of meaningful interactions with patients. Empathy is recognized as a core human value in health care (International Charter for Human Values in Healthcare, Human Dimensions of Care Working Group, 2013) and is now accepted as an important component of patient satisfaction and recovery (Pollak et al., 2011; Riess, Kelley, Bailey, Konowitz, & Gray, 2011), patient adherence to care regimens, and patient belief in the value of the treatment (Hojat et al., 2011; Morse, Edwardsen, & Gordon, 2008). And yet even with such wide-ranging support, clinicians often fail to consider empathic interventions as a central component of their patient care. In fact, ". . . healthcare providers frequently fail to recognize the emotional and social problems their patients face, like depression or a lack of information about their condition, which can demoralize them and hinder their treatment" (Kalb, 2008, p. 46).

Although the mandate for, and value of, empathic care is clear, there remains some debate about how to fully cultivate it as a clinical skill. How can it be effectively taught? Does it dissipate as clinicians become more stressed and time constraints grow tighter? Are empathy and compassion—empathy being the capacity for sensing and understanding another person's distress, and compassion being the willingness to convey that understanding through an action to alleviate the distress—inseparable?

Empathy Defined

Part of the problem in understanding, teaching, and endorsing empathy as a central core skill may be due to inconsistencies in its definition, measurement, and isolation. Rousseau (2008) examined concepts of empathy, and drawing from the *Oxford Medical Dictionary* and his own impressions, described it as "the ability to understand the thoughts and emotions of another person, or in other words, imagining how it feels to be in another person's situation"(Rousseau, 2008, p. 261). He goes on to clarify that empathy is not the same as sympathy, where an individual actually *feels* the emotions of another person. This definition of empathy emphasizes the clinician's *understanding* of a patient's emotions. It seems, then, that empathy is the first part of the equation for compassion: The clinician's understanding of patient emotion then prompts the clinician to act in a manner to provide help. Empathy, coupled with an effort to alleviate suffering, equals compassion.

Even though empathy is now understood to be a critical component of helping relationships that is strongly associated with patient satisfaction and recovery, it is not often explicitly defined in research projects. There seems to be little agreement on its scope, and the term is often used interchangeably with references appearing more consistent with descriptions of sympathy and compassion. Confusion also exists around the *experience* of empathy versus its *expression*. Clinicians may possess empathy—that is, they *understand* the thoughts and emotions of a patient—but the patient cannot benefit from that understanding unless the clinician also has the skills necessary to actually *convey* empathy to the patient. After all, if the patient doesn't sense that he or she has been heard and understood, then empathy may have little utility as far as the patient's recovery is concerned.

Whether empathy can be taught remains a subject of debate. Is it an innate ability to understand others, or can clinicians acquire this particular capacity through education? With more credibility being given to empathy, there has been a renewed interest in identifying effective methods of promoting it. Teaching initiatives are producing some promising results. Projects like the physician-focused Comskil initiative use both didactic and role-play methods to enhance physician communication skills so that physicians can more effectively express empathy in a manner that patients can readily experience (Touchpoints, 2008).

Mindfulness principles can also be used to help clinicians more effectively develop empathy. Utilizing a mindfulness framework, we can both promote empathy in ourselves and learn to express that empathy effectively to our patients. The first step is to stop, reflect, and consider the patient's experience. This means to transcend one's own needs, and to step into the shoes of the patient—to imagine what it must be like for this patient to be in this illness predicament. Once imagined, then it is useful to form hypotheses about the patient's experience and to be willing to test whether these hypotheses are accurate. Finally, when interacting with the patient, it is crucial to use the encounter to seek to understand what the illness experience is like for *this* patient. This is done primarily through the use of open-ended questions, with an awareness of the kinds of issues that similar patients often face.

After the patient has had a chance to "tell his or her story" and share his or her perspective, the clinician has an opportunity, via validation and acknowledgment, to express empathy toward the patient. In this second step, where the clinician is conveying empathy, there is also an opportunity to transmit a sense that the patient's suffering is important. This sounds simple, but in actual practice, it requires considerable ability to fully attend to the patient's distress. To understand a patient's emotional experience requires a willingness to explore it, through a series of questions, and to guide the patient through the process of describing his or her experience, and then to validate to the patient that his or her suffering matters. Applying our own hunches as to what the experience must be like for the patient misses the mark. Seeing the experience from the patient's perspective is paramount.

Clinical Example

Henry Wallingford (Mr. W) is a 70-year-old man who has recently undergone major abdominal surgery for perforated diverticulitis. He has an infected wound that has not healed in spite of the use of several antibiotics. He has been hospitalized for 3 months, in a hospital that is over 100 miles from his home, making it difficult for his wife of 45 years to visit. The nurse, Greta Michaels, having read through Mr. W's chart and heard about how frustrated he is becoming with his stalled recovery, has used mindfulness skills in preparing for this encounter.

Application of Mindfulness

Greta, applying a dual-awareness perspective, considers Mr. W's potential thoughts, feelings, and needs before she even enters his room. She realizes that Mr. W is far from home and disappointed at his lack of progress. She hypothesizes that he might be feeling isolated from friends and family and other sources of social support. She wonders if perhaps he may be beginning to question the likelihood of cure, or that he may fear death. She also realizes that Mr. W might express his emotions with anger because it is common for people who are feeling vulnerable and who may have lost trust in their care providers to use anger as a means of expressing their concerns. Greta then examines her own thoughts, feelings, and needs. Using the four mind states model (Chapter 2) as a frame of reference, she assesses that she has been able to use Reason Mind to consider Mr. W's perspective, that the (Body Mind) butterflies in her stomach may be a manifestation of her anxiety in potentially having to deal with an angry patient, and that her examination of Emotion Mind has helped her to acknowledge that she is anxious about having to be the one to hang yet another IV antibiotic for a potentially angry, sad, and understandably frustrated patient who might very well verbally lash out at her, just because she is the most available target for his malcontent. Going back into Wise Mind, Greta reminds herself that she cannot fix Mr. W's situation. She cannot magically make the new antibiotic more effective, or instantly heal his wound, even if she'd like to. But she can give him her concern, convey her understanding, and transmit to him her sense that his suffering matters, and that she feels for him in that suffering. With these thoughts in mind, and with a determination to meet *his* needs, not hers, she walks toward the room. Mr. Wallingford sees her coming.

Mr. W: Oh great, now what? Haven't you all tortured me enough?

[Greta responds by describing the new medication's actions.]
Greta: You sound frustrated. I know you had been hopeful that the previous antibiotic would work and that you'd be home by now.
[She doesn't get defensive or try to meet his criticisms with argument counterpoints. She accepts, and is open to listening to, his frustration.]

Mr. W: Who wouldn't be frustrated? You people keep telling me that the next antibiotic will be the one that heals this wound but so far, nothing's worked!

Greta: You're right, nothing has worked yet. [Greta agrees, joining with the patient, not trying to deny or spin reality in a falsely cheerful way.]

Mr. W: How am I supposed to get out of here when nothing that you are doing is making any difference? Sometimes it seems like I'll never get out of here.

Greta: I can see how you might think that. It must be discouraging when you get your hopes up and then the antibiotic doesn't do what we'd hoped it would. [Greta is identifying Mr. W's feelings and, by rephrasing his words, demonstrating that she understands.]

Mr. W: How am I supposed to keep going? This seems pointless.

Greta: It's perfectly understandable that you might begin to feel hopeless. You've been through a lot with this illness, the surgery, and now the infection. It is the kind of situation that wears people down. [She is validating his perspective.]

Mr. W: [less angry] You know I've always been so active. Before this, I was involved in my church, played cards with my buddies, tinkered around in the garage. Now, all I do is lie in this bed and count the hours going by.

Greta: Mr. Wallingford, I don't blame you for feeling fed up with all of this waiting. And while you're waiting, time passes slowly. I can't make it go any faster, but I can try to help make this hospital experience a little less difficult for you. What kinds of things do you enjoy doing at home that we may be able to replicate here in the hospital? Is there a hobby or pastime that you could tap into while you are here—maybe by accessing some resources via the Internet?

Only after having fully validated Mr. W's feelings and expressing empathy for his situation does Greta then move into problem-solving mode. Clinicians frequently make the mistake of moving into problem-solving prematurely. Doing so often escalates the patient's anger because it seems to dishonor the depth of the patient's concerns. Greta was careful to listen, empathize, and convey that empathy through her restatements of the patient's words, then to validate his emotions and, only then, move on to problem solving. Again, although these steps may seem obvious, when feeling time pressured or anxious, or when focused on concrete approaches to fixing problems rather than first addressing the emotional needs of patients, even

very skilled clinicians can seem oblivious to the importance of taking these steps in the necessary sequence.

Empathy and Mindfulness

Critical to this interchange is the fact that Greta allows
Mr. W to ventilate his feelings first. Then she accepts his
emotions and empathizes with him. And only after that
does she attempt to move toward some kind of intervention. So often well-meaning clinicians try to "fix" what
they see as the problem, before taking the time to fully "be"
with the patient's suffering and understand it, from the
patient's perspective. To honor a patient's experience, to listen, validate, empathize, and accept the patient's thoughts
and feelings, requires a deliberate mindful stance, one of
being open to, and finding value in, such efforts and to
consider empathy-based activities as central to the clinician's role (not just as occasional forays into the suffering
of the most compelling patients).

Greta cannot cure Mr. W's illness, but through her willingness to offer her time and attention, actively listen to his
issues, encourage him to ventilate feelings and concerns,
tolerate her own anxiety in the face of his anger, accept the
sadness she feels at the potentially poor outcome he might
experience, and validate his concerns and express understanding of his situation, she eases his suffering. Her empathy allows Mr. W to heal emotionally, if even temporarily.
And that easing of suffering matters.

At first glance, Greta's expression of empathy for Mr. W
seems simple—mostly just passive listening—but in fact
it required deliberate preparation, conscious analysis and
effort, and the application of skills gained through practice. First, Greta had to remember the value of empathy,

of being empathic, of expressing empathy and the healing impact it can have for patients. Next, she had to engage in mindful practice. Once she had moved into a mindful frame of reference she could work through a mental model, where she:

1. Conducted an assessment of her current internal climate
2. Examined her thoughts and emotions and held them up to scrutiny
3. Scanned her body to identify physical manifestations of her emotional state
4. Considered her patient's potential thoughts, feelings, and needs
5. Entered her own Wise Mind, acknowledging that she needed to transcend her own needs, at least for now, in order to address the needs of the patient
6. Did this with a willingness to tolerate her own distressing emotions in order to offer sensitive and effective care

References

Hojat, M., Louis, D. Z., Markham, F. W., Wender, R., Rabinowitz, C., & Gonnella, J. S. (2011). Physicians' empathy and clinical outcomes for diabetic patients. *Academic Medicine: Journal of the Association of American Medical Colleges, 86*(3), 359–364. doi: 10.1097/ACM.0b013e3182086fe1

International Charter for Human Values in Healthcare, Human Dimensions of Care Working Group. (2013). *The International Charter for Human Values in Healthcare.* Retrieved January 20, 2014, from http://charterforhealthcarevalues.org

Kalb, C. (2008, June 23). Health for life. The doctor factor. Doctors and patients who battle cancer together can develop a unique bond: Corned beef on chemo day. *Newsweek, 151*(25), 44, 46, 48.

Morse, D. S., Edwardsen, E. A., & Gordon, H. S. (2008). Missed opportunities for interval empathy in lung cancer communication. *Archives of Internal Medicine, 168*(17), 1853–1858. doi: 10.1001/archinte.168.17.1853

Pollak, K. I., Alexander, S. C., Tulsky, J. A., Lyna, P., Coffman, C. J., Dolor, R. J., . . . Østbye, T. (2011). Physician empathy and listening: Associations with patient satisfaction and autonomy. *The Journal of the American Board of Family Medicine, 24*(6), 665–672.

Riess, H., Kelley, J. M., Bailey, R., Konowitz, P. M., & Gray, S. T. (2011). Improving empathy and relational skills in otolaryngology residents: A pilot study. *Otolaryngology—Head and Neck Surgery, 144*(1), 120–122.

Rousseau, P. (2008). Empathy. *The American Journal of Hospice & Palliative Care, 25*(4), 261–262. doi: 10.1177/1049909108315524

Touchpoints. (2008). A newsletter of the Kenneth B. Schwartz Center (pp. 1–3). Retrieved from http://www.theschwartzcenter.org

Listening 4

There is perhaps no other interpersonal skill that is so simple and yet so difficult as listening. Listening is an obvious and often overlooked aspect of high-quality patient care. To actively listen means that the clinician has to stop talking. This is hard. Talking is how we convey important information. It's how we provide advice and perspective. It's how we deliver our diagnosis or our impression. To stop talking may feel uncomfortable, almost as if we've stopped doing our job. It becomes second nature to fill the interactional spaces with information. And information is what we know best. It's what is at our fingertips.

Listening requires the kind of focused attention that can be challenging to cultivate. It requires clinicians to make a deliberate shift away from our usual ways of functioning in our *modus operandi*. Listening isn't just an absence of talk, where we merely stand by silently until the patient finishes speaking so that we can jump in and tend to the next question on our checklist. It means fully, deeply, and attentively attending to patients' efforts to deliver their thoughts and ideas. We are listening not for information alone, but for understanding. We are attempting to get a sense of what it is like for this patient to experience his or her illness within the context of this patient's life circumstances. To attentively listen requires that we be fully present in the here and now, focused on the patient and only the patient, and able to put other concerns aside, at least for the moment.

Given the environment in which modern health care is provided, the ability to stop, shift, and turn one's full attention to a patient and family, to their thoughts, feelings, and needs, means having to temporarily "turn off and tune out" all manner of distractions. Beepers, monitors, overhead pages, call bells, intercoms, cell phones, and computers consistently pull us away from our focus. But focus is exactly what we need to use in order to fully listen. Being able to focus is a core aspect of mindfulness. And focus is difficult to maintain. During any given interaction the clinician will feel pulled to shift attention to pagers and computers and call bells, but maintaining focus on the patient is a decision to observe the distractions but not engage them, to acknowledge that distractions are present in the environment but to deliberately escort one's attention back to what the patient is saying.

To engage in quality listening is a commitment, made over and over again, in the service of effective patient care. That commitment can be reinforced when we remember that in order for the clinician to convey empathy, the patient has to be heard and understood. The "being heard" part of the process comes first, and to be heard, a patient has to be deeply, fully, thoughtfully listened to. We need to remember that the sense of being heard can, by itself, provide considerable comfort.

The clinician who extends an offer to listen may initially surprise many patients. Often patients and family members are accustomed to keeping their thoughts and feelings contained, fearful that expressing them might upset or burden their providers. Fear of being perceived as difficult or as an imposition keeps many patients silent. Fear of being disliked or abandoned by a provider keeps other patients silent. Vulnerable patients who express doubt about the suitability of their treatment or question the clinician's opinion run considerable risk of being marginalized or treated with dismissive indifference.

Conversely, having the sense that their thoughts, feelings, and ideas are valued and important to the care process provides patients and families with the permission they need to more freely express their concerns, and in doing so, feel respected, valued, and included in the health care process. When a patient challenges a provider's perspective, conclusion, or diagnosis, the clinician needs to honor that challenge; have the emotional maturity and humility to use the patient's concerns as data; and be willing, if appropriate, to reconsider, revise, or altogether scrap a plan of care. Care is an ongoing, flexible process of modification, renegotiation, and cooperation, where patient and clinicians work as members of a team toward an identified goal. None of this is possible if clinicians aren't listening.

The Mindfulness of Listening

In Reason Mind, most clinicians recognize the need for and value of listening, but oftentimes Emotion Mind forces get activated early on in an encounter, impatience takes hold, and before the clinician can see it happening, he or she is operating from habitual patterns of firing off questions and interrupting patient answers in order to redirect the communication process in a very specific direction. Much of this need to take over and direct comes from a fear that if the clinician uses a less-structured questioning format combined with attentive listening, this will invite the patient to talk excessively and tangentially, leading the discussion in irrelevant directions and wasting time. Or, that if too many issues emerge, the clinician will have difficulty knowing how to exit the encounter gracefully. Or, if emotionally sensitive issues emerge, these will cause the clinician to feel more uncomfortable, or ill equipped to knowledgeably handle the complexity of the patient's suffering. If clinicians are blind to these anxieties and they remain undetected, well-meaning providers can easily become wary of listening and use interruption as a means of controlling how much distress patients reveal.

If the clinician also has to contend with a chronic sense of being rushed, with an agitated state of lingering urgency to move through interventions at a quick pace, this Body Mind agitation will interfere with even the best intentions to listen. In Wise Mind, clinicians observe, describe, and acknowledge these barriers and make conscious decisions to engage patients in effective interpersonal encounters in spite of internal forces that are prompting us to do just the opposite. With mindfulness, we take notice that our attention is drifting, and then we decide, again and again, to escort our focus back to what the patient is saying. This is how old habits give way to new (Goleman, 2013). Not every encounter needs to include a conference where sensitive issues are discussed, but every encounter needs to include an invitation for the patient to express his or her most compelling issues, be they pain, lack of information, frustration, hopelessness, and the like. And for those patients who do express more complex, emotionally sensitive concerns, these can be greeted with acceptance rather than avoidance.

Although listening does take time, often it is not as much time as people imagine. In fact, when health care practitioners (HCPs) turn their full attention to patients, and set aside just a few minutes to really listen, they often find that this facilitates, rather than obstructs, effective time use during the encounter. Use of more open-ended interviewing techniques, where patients are actually encouraged to talk, can elicit a wealth of critical information from patients that serves multiple purposes, providing concrete relevant information while simultaneously helping to establish rapport. It can help to mitigate situations where the patient waits until the physician or nurse is done, then expresses a serious or complex need that could have been addressed earlier in the encounter had its expression been invited.

Commonly, clinicians avoid soliciting patient concerns for fear that the patient will become emotionally fragile and "needy" and the clinician will feel inadequate in attempting to address the patient's concern. This fear is often based on a "fix-it" assumption within the provider. Socialized to be in a role that provides help and cure, many clinicians believe that it is their primary responsibility to fix whatever problem the patient brings. This underlying assumption about the nature of health care, although admirable on the one hand, can also predispose the clinician to both unrealistic expectations of himself or herself and ineffective care of the patient. No one can fix death, for example. It is a part of every life journey. It can be delayed, but not avoided. If patients and families become sad, tearful, even angry at the news that death is the likely outcome, the clinician's role is to allow them to express their feelings, share their thoughts, and relay their needs. Those needs often include a desire to be heard, understood, and valued. Every clinician has the capacity to provide this kind of care. This is not a problem to be solved, just heard and understood.

The Basics

Listening is facilitated when clinicians sit down at eye level with patients, maintain appropriate eye contact (sensitive to cultural variations), and assume an unhurried demeanor. This conveys real interest and respect. The message to the patient is: "I want to know what this illness experience is like for you and am ready to honor the thoughts and feelings you describe."

Acknowledging that distractions are everywhere and consciously, deliberately choosing to ignore their pull requires a willingness to bring attention back, over and over again, to the patient. Deliberately keeping pagers and phones in pockets or holsters, even when they sound, keeps the focus on the patient. Except in rare circumstances, devices can be checked later.

When much of the encounter has to be captured on a computer, it is critical for the clinician to inform the patient of what to expect: "Mr. Stubbs, I will be moving through a few quick questions that I need to be sure we cover and that are listed on this computer screen. Once I've completed the list I will turn my full attention to you and discuss whatever is on your mind. I want to hear about how things have been going for you."

Dual Awareness

Many patient issues or concerns can be anticipated if practitioners are able to employ the dual-awareness framework discussed in Chapter 2. Being able to anticipate the thoughts, feelings, and needs of patients and families allows the provider to expect that these will emerge, and by soliciting open dialog, address these important aspects of care.

Clinical Example

Timothy Hopkins (Mr. H) is a 74-year-old patient on the hospital's Rehabilitation Unit. He suffered a stroke 4 weeks ago and has been on rehab for the past 3 weeks, learning to walk with a cane and trying to feed and dress himself in the face of his residual hemiparesis. He is now ambulatory but continues to require considerable assistance with dressing and bathing. He has some moderate expressive aphasia, which causes his speech to be slow and deliberate. His rehab physician, the unit social worker, and the rehab primary nurse have called a family meeting to discuss discharge plans for Mr. H. In attendance are the patient's wife Edith, a 70-year-old woman who suffers from osteoarthritis; Timothy and Edith's daughter Susan, an attorney who lives 500 miles away and has flown in to attend the meeting but is staying only 48 hours; and Timothy and Edith's son Tim Jr., a local teacher, who has been trying to help manage his parents' affairs. Nick, the physician, begins the meeting by making introductions and reviewing the purpose of the gathering: to formalize Mr. H's discharge arrangements. Nick explains that the Rehab Unit has worked hard to help Mr. H regain as much of his functioning as possible but that he has residual deficits that will take time to improve. He recommends that Mr. H be transferred to an extended care facility where he can have some on-site physical therapy and where attendants can address his needs for feeding and bathing. Nick emphasizes that Mrs. H's arthritis makes it impossible for her to care for her husband at home and that the facility is the best option for adequate care. Susan agrees that this seems to be the best option, and when her mother protests, Susan responds to her by saying: "Mom, you want Dad to have the best care, don't you?" Margo, the nurse, confirms that Mr. H is not yet able to take a shower on his own, or to use a fork and knife effectively, and given Mrs. H's limitations, needs outside help. Tim Jr. is aware that his father, a normally quiet man who is very self-sufficient and rarely asks for help, would need to have help imposed on him in order to get adequate care.

In all of this, Mr. H is not directly addressed. The rehab team is delivering the information to the family and not making eye contact with the patient. When he tries to speak, Susan tells her father that he need not concern himself with the discussion, that she will ask all the right questions and make sure he gets the care he needs. This meeting is conducted with speed and efficiency: The team members report their findings, inform the family of their conclusions, and move the discussion toward steps to secure a bed for Mr. H at the extended care facility.

Suddenly, Mr. H becomes agitated and angry. He is trying to speak when Tim Jr. interrupts and says, "Dad, it's okay. I know you are worried about Mom but I'll look in on her; I'll help her with groceries and meals. You just concentrate on getting better." Mr. H then throws his cane on the ground and pounds his fist on the wheelchair armrest. He attempts to speak. Shocked, the physician turns to the family and begins to explain that sometimes after a stroke, patients can get easily frustrated and have poor frustration tolerance. The social worker, Betty, politely asks that everyone stop talking. She turns to Mr. Hopkins and says: "Mr. Hopkins, we've been talking *about* you, but not *with* you and yet this decision affects you much more than any of us. Please take your time and tell us what you think about all this." Very slowly and with slurred speech, Mr. H explains that he doesn't want to go to the extended care facility, but before he can finish conveying his thoughts, the nurse interrupts with "But Mr. Hopkins, you know that your wife can't take care of you at home. . . ." The social worker interrupts Margo and refocuses the attention back to Mr. H. She says "Mr. Hopkins, please tell us more. It's your turn to talk and we are here to listen." Nick, the physician, glances at his watch and looks at a piece of paper, his "to-do" list, that he pulls from his lab coat pocket. Margo, the nurse, looks away, her foot impatiently tapping beneath the conference room table. In the meantime, Mr. H slowly, painstakingly attempts to convey that he wants to go home, that he wants physical therapy and home health attendants to come to his home to help, and that more than anything else, he wants to remain with his wife. He says he has money saved up if insurance won't pay for the care. He says that he understands that his wishes represent a plan that is different from what everyone else wants but he has made up his mind. He conveys to the group his understanding that staying at home might put him at risk for falls or further complications of his stroke but that he takes full responsibility for that risk.

When Nick begins to take issue with Mr. H and provide counterpoint arguments against this alternate plan, Betty reminds Nick that it is the patient who determines the goals of care, and that as long as Mr. H holds the cognitive capacity to make his own health care decisions, the decision rests with him. Betty is listening. She understands that for Mr. H, the *quality* of his life is more important than the *quantity*. She accepts that while Mr. H's plan is not ideal, that it does place him at higher risk for falls and other accidents, and that he might not get the level of care that would be most appropriate, it is what Mr. H wants. Betty also recognizes that it is possible for Mr. H to receive services at home and it is possible for Mr. H to hire services in addition to those that are covered by Medicare. She understands that sometimes when people are transferred to extended care facilities against their wishes, they sometimes fail to improve. Betty has listened; she has used the information that Mr. H revealed and has tried to imagine what it is like to be in his shoes. She listened with a willingness to consider what this situation must be like for this patient at this time. She understands his concerns and her actions are informed by that understanding. She realizes that by supporting Mr. H she will be in opposition to the wishes of the patient's children and to the other team members, but she also knows that, in the end, it is the patient who is the focus of their efforts.

Reference

Goleman, D. (2013). *Curing the common cold of leadership: Poor listening.* Retrieved January 24, 2014, from http://www.linkedin.com/today/post/article/20130502140433-117825785-curing-the-common-cold-of-leadership-poor-listening

Words 5

*I*n the preceding chapters, the reader has been challenged to consider the value of mindfulness as a framework for clinical practice. From a mindful perspective, health care providers can operate with greater focus and attention, and with a consistent orientation toward enhancing patient encounters. Within a mindful approach, we can rebalance our inner experience and soothe our own emotional landscape so that our energy can be directed outward toward the thoughts, feelings, and needs of patients and families. When we are better positioned to convey interest, acceptance, availability, and a desire to understand, we can then select effective words and phrases that invite patients to share their concerns.

The table provided later in this chapter outlines techniques that have been used for decades to elicit patient disclosure. Although examples of their use are listed to provide clarity, it is understood that each of us has our own communication style, and within that individual style, a set of words, expressions, and idioms that are consistent with it. That said, it is important to remember that sometimes within our health care culture we adopt words and phrases that outsiders have difficulty translating. Clarity and precision in conveying information remain important goals in any interaction. For example, when the wife of an acutely ill man with pancreatitis is provided with the instruction "Given the potential for further complications, I'd have a low threshold for admission, should his condition worsen," she may be at a loss to understand exactly what this means. Simpler, more explicit language would be more likely to decrease the wife's anxiety and confusion and increase her understanding: "If his fever increases, he is in more pain, or he just looks worse, bring him in to the emergency department so that we can determine if he needs to be admitted to the hospital."

From a mindfulness-based perspective, the physician would anticipate the thoughts, feelings, and needs of an anxious wife, struggling to manage her husband's care at home. The physician would remember that when feeling anxious, people are much less able to interpret nuances in communication and they do better with specific direction, especially when dealing with unfamiliar circumstances. Understanding of the wife's anxiety and how her anxiety may interfere with her ability to interpret vague language would prompt the physician to provide clear, more concrete direction.

There is a time and place to use open-ended questions to elicit from patients (and family members) their beliefs, concerns, and emotions. There is also a time when being clear, concrete, and specific, using language and terminology that patients can easily understand, is equally as important. Clinician use of jargon remains a major barrier to clear communication and leads to considerable misunderstanding, patient nonadherence, and interpersonal conflict. Telling the patient that he must remain NPO (nothing orally/by mouth) after midnight may make perfect sense to health care professionals, but the patient may have no idea what this means. Is it the patient's responsibility to ask? No. People don't ask because they may feel stupid, because they think they know what a term means, or because they sense the clinician's hurriedness. When the patient presents for his procedure but he's eaten breakfast and the procedure is canceled, the schedule is disrupted, the clinicians become frustrated, and there's often an effort to assign blame for the mishap. Usually the blame falls squarely on the patient, which is not only unfair, but significantly undermines the patient's trust in the services and satisfaction with care. Ultimately, it is the patient who suffers.

As clinicians, it is our obligation to use a more mindful approach, to be ever sensitive to the need to use our words as precision instruments through which we convey thoughts, ideas, and information in a manner that is most effective for patients. When we are focused on their needs, with the capacity to perceive those needs from the patients' perspective, we are better equipped to translate our instructions, insights, or information in a way that has the greatest potential to be useful to patients.

No discussion of therapeutic communication is complete without taking a look at the kinds of phrases that can disrupt or undermine a patient–clinician encounter. Part Two: Nontherapeutic Communication in the following table provides examples of such phrases. Some of the examples listed might seem obviously insensitive, whereas with others, their negative impact is more nuanced. For example, clinicians might feel quite comfortable using praise to try to reinforce patient behaviors that are seen as positive and compliant with treatment, but sometimes these expressions of praise can seem patronizing or paternalistic, as if the patient is complying with treatment recommendations primarily for the purpose of pleasing the clinician rather than because it is in the patient's own best interest to do so.

It is more effective for the clinician who, for example, wants to encourage a patient to continue to exhibit effective technique when changing her own wound dressings to say something like, "That is exactly the kind of quality wound care that will help to get that incision healed up quickly. It seems you've got a good grasp of the technique," rather than "I'm so glad that you are doing such a great job."

Another ineffective technique is the use of questions that begin with *why*. Asking "why" seems innocuous enough, but when used in certain circumstances it can be interpreted as a demand for an explanation, often from a patient who doesn't have a viable explanation to offer. For example, "Why did you stick your hand down the garbage disposal without turning it off first?" and "Why didn't you call the ambulance as soon as you experienced the chest pain?" are examples of questions that patients can interpret as indirect attempts at scolding them for irresponsible behavior rather than as efforts to gain information.

Words or phrases that challenge a patient's beliefs can be harmful as well, as can abrupt changes in topic or focus. Mindful communication keeps compassion at the forefront of clinician goals: to obtain information while extending empathy and concern. It helps to guide clarification efforts, including word choice, and brings sensitivity for the patient's perspective to the forefront of the encounter. Being able to explore the patient's perspective helps clinicians orient their interview and assessment processes to using the kinds of therapeutic communication techniques that both elicit important diagnostic information while providing opportunities to explore problems or concerns and address emotionally sensitive content. On the following pages the reader will find a brief summary of therapeutic and nontherapeutic communication techniques. Examples are provided to illustrate the all-too-common ways that we, as clinicians, can either enhance or detract from our efforts to use words effectively.

Therapeutic and Nontherapeutic Communication

PART ONE: THERAPEUTIC COMMUNICATION

A. Superficial Methods	Examples
Silence	Maintaining eye contact, leaning forward toward patient, facial expression reflecting interest
Listening	Nodding head "yes," saying "uh huh"
Recognition	"Hello, Mrs. Randolph [use the patient's name]. I see that you were able to do all of your wound care today."
Offering self	"I would like to sit and talk with you for a while."
Broad openings	"How have you been coping with all of this?"
	"What has you so worried?"
General leads	"Go on." "Then what happened?" "And now?"
Stating observations	"You seem preoccupied."
	"I notice that you are wringing your hands."
Requesting descriptions	"What thoughts are going through your mind?"
	"What are the obstacles to getting what you need?"
Restating	Patient: "I can't deal with this; I'm so overwhelmed."
	Physician: "You are feeling overwhelmed."
Reflecting	Patient: "Do you think I should move to a retirement facility?"
	Nurse: "Do *you* think you should?"

(*continued*)

(*continued*)

B. Deeper Methods	Examples
Giving information	"My name is _____."
	"For the next 15 to 20 minutes, I'd like to review your treatment."
Presenting reality	"I don't see your prognosis as being so negative."
	"That sound is an airplane traveling over the hospital."
	"I am the nurse working with you today. Your sister is not here."
Exploring	"Tell me more about that."
	"Could you describe that incident in more detail?"
	"What kind of work do you do?"
Seeking clarification	"I want to be sure I fully understand your concern. Would you tell me more about it?"
	"You've mentioned several concerns. Which ones are the most important for us to be sure to discuss today?"

C. Promoting Insight	Examples
Encouraging evaluation	"Do you think your anxiety interferes with your work performance?"
	"Do the demands of the job end up contributing to your sense of distress?"
Voicing doubt	"That has not been my experience."
	"Most people would not describe it that way."
Verbalizing the implied	Patient: "It's useless. Nothing I do makes a difference."
	Nurse: "You feel powerless to change your circumstances."
	Patient: "My boss thinks I'm an idiot, just like my wife does."
	Nurse: "You have a sense of being undervalued by important people in your life."

(*continued*)

(continued)

Attempting to translate into feelings	Patient: "I'm no good."
	Nurse: "Are you saying that you feel shame for past behaviors?"
	Patient: "I'm a woman without a country."
	Nurse: "Do you mean that you feel like you don't belong, that you are moving through your life alone?"
Summarizing	Clinician: "Let me review the main points of our discussion."
Encouraging formulation of a plan of action	Nurse practitioner: "Now that you've read through the material on diabetes management, do you have some ideas about measures that you could take that might help get your blood sugar under better control?"
	Nurse: "When your physician comes in, what thoughts do you have about how you might begin to tell him about your concerns?"

PART TWO: NONTHERAPEUTIC COMMUNICATION

A. Casual or Unperceptive Methods	Examples
Rejecting	"I don't think that needs to be discussed."
False reassurance	"Don't worry, it will all work out."
	"Everything will be alright."
	"God doesn't give people more hardship than they can handle."
Stereotypical remarks (aka clichés)	"I'm fine. How are you?"
	"It's all for the best."
Belittling or minimizing concerns	"Don't worry yourself about that."
	"Everyone feels that way sometimes."
	"God doesn't give us more hardship than we can handle."

(continued)

(*continued*)

A. Casual or Unperceptive Methods	Examples
Unrelated topic	Patient: "I am feeling so frustrated today." Nurse: "Have you seen today's news about the snow headed our way?"
Blunted responsiveness	Patient stops speaking and clinician fails to respond. Patient provides cue: "I'm just feeling so depressed." Clinician then looks down and checks clipboard in lap without responding.

B. Guiding or Directing Methods	Examples
Approval (conveying personal opinion or values)	"I am glad you did that." "That's great!"
Disapproval (conveying personal opinion or values)	"You should not have done that." "It's wrong to. . ."
Agree	"Yes, that is what you should do."
Disagree	"No, that's incorrect. You should not. . ."
Advise	"You should. . ." "You have to. . ."

C. Threatening or Ineffective Methods	Examples
Probe	"But how did you really feel?" "There must have been more to it than that."
Denial of problem	"No, that's not what you are really worried about." "You can't focus on that; we need to move on."
Test	"Do you realize what time it is?" "Do you know your name?"

(*continued*)

(*continued*)

C. Threatening or Ineffective Methods	Examples
Personal	"You need to do this for me."
	"Can you count to 10 for me?"
	"I will be held accountable if you don't comply with taking your medication."
Requesting explanation	"Why did you do it?"
	"Why is she so important to you?"
Interpreting	"You really don't know how to care for yourself adequately but are too embarrassed to admit it."
	"You don't care enough to put the energy into complying with treatment."
	"Unconsciously, you want to. . ."

Reference

Hays, J., & Larson, K. (1963). *Interacting with patients.* New York, NY: Macmillan & Co.

Patients' Emotions 6

Skilled clinicians pride themselves in their knowledge of diseases and treatments. Having an extensive command of anatomy and physiology, pharmacology, and the latest evidence-based breakthroughs is critical to providing competent care. But just as important is the knowledge of how illness can impact patient emotions. And although there is certainly room for individual variation, typical emotional reactions can often be anticipated. Having a sense of the normal emotions that accompany phases and stages of illness allows clinicians to think about how to incorporate the emotional domain into patient assessments and plans of care. Working with patients' emotions, from a place of understanding and acceptance, allows the clinician to tactfully address the emotions in a manner that best serves the patients' needs. To do this well requires clinician mindfulness.

Anticipating a patient's emotions is part of clinician mindfulness practice. With a dual-awareness perspective, the clinician is both paying attention to his or her own agenda while anticipating the likely thoughts, feelings, and needs of the patient. But so often, because of the emphasis on expertise in attending to a patient's physical needs, the emotional needs get lost. And although the last decade has seen more emphasis on holistic, or patient-centered, care, there remain major gaps in clinicians' willingness to embrace their role in mitigating patients' emotional distress. Clearly, clinicians cannot serve as psychotherapists or mental health counselors—this is beyond their scope and focus—but every clinician can provide the kind of emotional support that is so much a part of empathic and compassionate care. Doing so requires a few relatively simple but ongoing steps.

First, it is critical to recognize and address one's own anxiety in witnessing, and being expected to effectively respond to, a patient's emotional distress. This anxiety often serves as the major impediment to effective care. Many clinicians will verbalize a sense of being too busy or too specially trained to deal with the personal nature of a patient's emotions, but this emotional distancing behavior often masks an underlying discomfort, perhaps with emotions in general. Emotions are part of every human experience. Illness is both a physical and an emotional phenomenon. These cannot be separated. And although physicians and nurses focus the majority of their training on the physical aspects of care, they cannot effectively treat patients without a basic understanding of, and ability to work with, patients' emotional responses.

Working effectively with patients' emotions, especially strong, negative emotions, is not a universal or innate skill, but before we can be effective in addressing patients' emotions, we need to acknowledge that emotions matter and that every clinician's compassionate practice includes a respect for, and a desire to work with, patients' emotions. Mindfulness practice can be very useful in decreasing our anxiety concerning emotions and can help to increase our awareness of, and effectiveness in, addressing the emotions that are inherent to physical illness. When operating from Reason Mind, we may be quite capable of identifying the emotional needs of patients, but once Emotion Mind begins to dominate our experience, it is easy to feel apprehensive and uncertain of our skill, and then avoid discussing emotions with patients. Wise Mind activation helps us to remember that we are not being asked to serve as psychotherapists—only to listen, to try to understand from the patient's perspective, to validate the patient's point of view (which is different from agreeing with it), and then, without judgment or defensiveness, to extend a willingness to continue to walk the illness journey with the patient.

A discussion of some of the more common patient emotions follows.

Fear

Illness, trauma, pain, and surgery are frightening experiences. They bring into conscious awareness our own vulnerability and our mortality. We take our health for granted until something happens that shakes our assumptions about ourselves, our world, and our future. When afraid, people often become irritable because fear is uncomfortable. They may make demands, sometimes rudely, in an effort to obtain relief. Sometimes clinicians misinterpret a patient's rude demands, taking the rudeness personally and becoming defensive or angry. Responding to this as a personal slight shifts the focus to the clinician's own needs and away from the patient's need for relief.

Grief

Grief is not just the domain of people who have lost loved ones. Illness imposes many alterations in a patient's physical and emotional integrity. Illness can rob people of their stamina, functional ability, and comfort. It can severely limit a patient's capability to move through life as he or she once did. Watching one's self become less mobile, more dependent, more homebound, less agile, less athletic, and so forth can take an enormous psychological toll, especially if these losses are long term or irreversible. Losing one's former sense of health and vitality or sexual attractiveness can leave a patient scrambling to redefine his or her sense of self and relocate his or her value and purpose in life. In diseases where lifestyle alterations are even more dramatic—such as when a person is forced to stop working, or confined to a wheelchair, or dependent on dialysis, or awaiting organ transplant—the stakes are even higher. The losses are enormous and the emotional toll is profound.

Sadness

Sadness can be deep and overwhelming. It can manifest as symptoms of a tight throat and tearful eyes, a heaviness that feels crushing, or sobbing that doesn't seem to stop. It can seem so deep that both patient and provider can feel helpless in its presence. And yet sadness is as common and natural as any other emotion. It serves to help us get in touch with our most elemental hopes and dreams, and the threat of losing them. And because it can cause distress, even alarm, in clinicians, there is an almost urgent need to fix it. Sometimes, well-meaning clinicians will interpret a patient's sadness as clinical depression, assuming that if a patient has a strong emotional reaction to learning about a serious or potentially terminal illness, that such sadness represents a manifestation of psychopathology. Witnessing a patient's sadness can create sadness and anxiety in the clinician, which lingers long after the encounter has ended.

Frustration

Many treatments require a trial-and-error approach. Patients are asked to purchase expensive medications and devices that may or may not work, for example. Often recovery can take time and a variety of interventions before a good fit is found and the patient begins to respond. Patients will likely be frustrated by this, especially if they do not understand the process or because of lack of information, and they can lose trust in their providers. Often, well-meaning clinicians become defensive in the face of patient frustration, defending the value of the treatment or the quality of their judgment. Clinicians get anxious in the face of treatment failure, and a frustrated patient often serves to aggravate clinicians' feelings of inadequacy or uncertainty.

Anger

Clinicians feel considerable distress in the face of overtly angry patients and/or families. In the helping professions, even the most seasoned and cavalier of providers has a sense of needing to be valued by patients. Much of the satisfaction that clinicians obtain from their work is in experiencing the positive regard and gratitude of those for whom they care. Clinicians often experience patient or family anger as the antithesis of such regard. And yet, if a clinician is able to stand back and look more objectively at a given patient's situation, more often than not, the reason for, or justification of, the anger is obvious. Illness is stressful. There are inherent indignities that patients experience even with our efforts to mitigate them. Patients have to contend with myriad of inconveniences, annoyances, lack of control, unpredictability, changing schedules, transient personnel, cold food, and the list goes on. So often, a patient's anger is taken personally by whoever is in the vicinity to receive it. And if the patient's anger results in Emotion Mind activation in the recipient, then without pulling back and observing the process, a clinician can react reflexively in a manner that only aggravates the situation. Interpersonal effectiveness in addressing anger can be very powerful, and can perhaps serve to fully convert disbelieving clinicians into embracing the power of mindfulness. Handled mindfully, with ego detachment and a resolve to express empathy, a clinician can help a patient feel heard, understood, and valued in a way that serves to dissipate the patient's anger and allow for constructive resolution with clinician and patient, instead of being enemies, feeling like they are back on the same team, working together toward a common goal.

Hopelessness

When treatment drags on and progress is slow or nonexistent, patients often experience a type of mental exhaustion that leaves them hopeless. Many professionals identify this as "giving up." Much of the literature on recovery in cancer treatment refers to patients staying in the fight, activating their resolve, and focusing their energy on fighting the cancer with courage and determination. Although this can be a useful metaphor, it can also backfire. At times, all the determination in the world won't change the course of an aggressive cancer. And in the face of treatment failure, patients who embraced the "fight" perspective can feel defeated, even betrayed by a system that seemed to have promised them that putting up a fight would result in a good outcome. These kinds of experiences evoke strong emotions. It is natural for patients to feel hopeless when chemotherapy or other treatments have failed to produce the desired results. Sometimes, when patients express feelings of hopelessness, health care providers can perceive this as an accusation, an indictment on the clinician's failure to provide the cure. If clinicians respond defensively, touting the research that points to the value of the treatment, they've missed a critical moment to validate the patient's right to feel hopeless, betrayed, frustrated, and afraid. To reinforce to the patient that such emotions are appropriate to the situation and that the clinician both understands these emotions and feels for the patient's suffering is an opportunity for the clinician to provide comfort and healing. Conversely, if the clinician responds with trite, stereotypical phrases about the patient needing to stay in the fight and not let the cancer win, this demeans the patient's concerns. It may serve the clinician, who doesn't feel comfortable in dealing with the patient's emotions, but it leaves the patient feeling both hopeless and alone in his or her suffering. The clinician doesn't need to, in that moment, fix the patient's perspective; the clinician just needs to be with it, be with the patient and stay present, focused on the patient and the patient's understandable distress.

Patients and families will have emotional reactions to illness and trauma and will need to express those reactions. The nature of that expression will vary according to a patient's personal style, ethnic and religious backgrounds, and personal comfort with the clinician. Addressing patient and family distress is part of every clinician's role because if the patient can express his or her feelings and concerns, openly, in an accepting and empathic encounter, the clinician is given a critical opportunity to honor that distress and provide the kind of support that allows the patient to heal.

Time

Several other chapters in this book address barriers that can diminish the quality of patient–provider encounters and damage patient–provider relationships. But perhaps the single most common one is time, or lack thereof. Most well-meaning clinicians value patients and hold themselves to standards of high-quality care but realize that certain constraints sometimes cause them to fall short. Working within modern health systems requires that clinicians comply with numerous record-keeping demands, many of which exist more for billing purposes than to document important findings or communicate care strategies. Gone are the days when the primary purpose of documentation was to provide a record that could be used and followed so as to provide continuity of care.

Ongoing and annual clinician training imposed to meet regulatory standards requires considerable clinician time and attention, especially for those of us who work within large health care systems. Time is being taken up by many activities that pull clinicians away from the bedside (or clinic exam table) and toward the computer screen. Given all the standard assessment questions that clinicians must ask their patients to be sure that all potential *physical* problems are uncovered, they often avoid delving into the psychosocial domain, even if doing so could inform the patients' care. Fearful that they might open a Pandora's box of issues, and that these issues may be emotionally burdensome and areas in which clinicians believe that they can offer little help, clinicians may altogether avoid tapping into the emotional aspects of their patients' illness experience. And yet, in many situations, it is just this kind of attention that humanizes a patient's care.

Much of patient adherence to medical treatment is determined by how much the treatment is understood by patients and families. If a medication is causing side effects, or a treatment requires considerable lifestyle adjustment, or clinic visits represent travel hardship, for example, patients may feel uncomfortable discussing this with a clinician who is preoccupied with moving through the encounter by checking items off a checklist. Patients may stop taking a medication, complying with a treatment, or attending clinic visits because whatever the obstacle is, they don't feel that the encounter allows for safe disclosure. Without understanding the contributing factors, when faced with "noncompliant" patients, clinicians may fall into a pattern of assigning negative judgments—such as "he is so lazy; he can't be bothered to fill his prescription"—and then becoming less invested in the patient's care.

For many clinicians, the pace of health care delivery leaves them feeling frazzled, harried, and, at times, exploited. Over time, the pace can seem so unrelenting that time itself becomes an enemy and the work becomes little more than a constant sprint. Patient care becomes something that is to be done as quickly and efficiently as possible. Connecting with patients may begin to take on a superficial, rote quality—polite, usually cheerful, but without a real attempt to listen, understand, and engage. Resentment builds as lunch breaks get missed and mandatory overtime is initiated in order to fill staffing gaps. Clinicians in these situations often limit their clinical focus to the tasks on check-off lists, leaving work as soon as possible, and investing their emotional energy elsewhere. This emotional disengagement comes at a price, as opportunities for human connection are lost and these once-dedicated, compassionate professionals are reduced to acting as technicians. This is an insidious process, so gradual that such clinicians are often unaware of the transition, until one day they notice that their passion for the work is gone.

In mindfulness, time is focused on the "here and now." Efficient use of the present moment combined with the principle of completing tasks one at a time can help clinicians remain focused. Often, much of the concrete information that clinicians need to complete the perfunctory aspects of care might actually be addressed spontaneously by patients when patients are encouraged to just talk about how they are doing with managing their care. When given a chance to express concerns openly, patients reveal all manner of issues and questions that can be effectively addressed. Any missing data can be obtained, via checklist, later in the visit, if necessary.

Mindful clinicians enter the patient's hospital room (or clinic exam room) having first taken 30 seconds to clear their minds, re-orient themselves to the present moment, commit themselves to being in the "here and now," and consider what the thoughts, needs, and feelings of the patient might be before they even enter the room. Time remains precious but the encounter is executed in a manner that allows for patient disclosure. For example: "Mr. MacMillan, I see from looking at your chart that you've lost weight. How have you been managing at home? Can you describe how you get your meals?" This kind of question allows for much richer discussion than if the physician asks: "Are you eating?" "What are you eating?" and follows up with: "How much are you eating? You need to start drinking Ensure."

Open-ended questions that express interest in the patient's lived experience need not take more time than the interrogation-style ones often used, and open-ended questions often elicit the kinds of information that the clinician is actually seeking.

But there are also situations that simply take time, that require sustained clinician attention, and that are not financially compensated. No attempts at increased efficiency will shorten these encounters: the sobbing patient who learns that her leg will have to be amputated, the bone marrow transplant patient who is at his wits' end as the prolonged confinement of his room begins to wreck havoc on his mental health, the woman who just learned of her breast cancer diagnosis and whose mind is so overwhelmed that she cannot process the instructions she's being given by the oncologist. These are the kinds of time-consuming situations that clinicians face daily and that cannot be truncated in order to meet strict time limits.

Nurses and physicians face intense moral conflict when they feel divided by equally compelling demands: the post-op patient who is in terrible pain waiting for the nurse to come into his room with the injection, while the dying patient asks for emotional comfort, and the patient being discharged has already been waiting for 2 hours to obtain the required wound care instruction—the last step in the discharge process that has to be completed before she can be cleared to leave the hospital, or the physician whose pager won't stop beeping as colleagues demand immediate consultations, clinic patients are waiting, trainees need advice and instruction, and, at the same time, she is being summoned to the procedure area where the patient has been prepped and the procedure is now running an hour late.

Time-pressured, competing demands are some of the most challenging job stressors that providers face. With every demand being equally urgent and compelling, the clinician is left with a "no-win" situation: To meet the needs of one patient (or colleague), another is left waiting, wanting, and dissatisfied. When scenarios like this happen occasionally, mindful practice can provide the clinician with the calm centeredness to get through them effectively. When such scenarios happen frequently, the onus of responsibility for change shifts from the individual clinician to the health care organization.

Although mindfulness can help soothe the battered soul of the harried nurse or the overextended physician, it too has it limits. It is only when mindfulness principles and commitments to compassion percolate through entire health care systems and more reasonable expectations are put in place that real change will occur. Some clinicians in some systems have been stretched to the very limits of their physical and mental health. Patient-centered–care commitments, touted in our institutions' mission statements, ring hollow in systems where clinician needs are ignored. System-based commitments to maintaining proper staffing ratios, providing adequate support personnel, implementing efficient processes, and supplying appropriate resources are critical workplace components for ethical and compassionate practice to prevail.

Boundaries 8

*P*rofessional boundaries are behavioral limits that are designed to protect a patient from even subtle forms of exploitation or harm. Because the role of "patient" places people in a position of great vulnerability, these professionally sanctioned limits provide an extra measure of safety, holding clinicians to a set of practice standards against which their efforts can be measured. Boundaries remind us that as professionals, we are bound by a kind of sacred trust.

Boundaries act as a set of principles that guide clinicians' behaviors so that within any given health care encounter, the focus of care remains exclusively on the *patient's* well-being. When we operate within professional boundaries, we act from compassion; we organize our efforts in a manner that preserves the patient's trust, while honoring the patient's dignity and attending to his or her suffering. We keep in confidence those aspects of a patient's life that are known to us solely by virtue of our professional role.

Maintaining professional boundaries means keeping our encounters patient-focused. The patient's concerns, feelings, and needs may be disclosed within the professional relationship, whereas the provider's personal concerns, feelings, and needs must be shared elsewhere, within his or her own social relationships with friends and colleagues, but not with patients. Boundary maintenance also includes honoring the patient's cultural norms and values, beliefs, and religious or philosophical foundations. It means being mindful of the reflex to pass judgment on a patient's behavior or lifestyle and being willing to extend an attitude of acceptance and respect for each patient's innate human value. To be fully effective, we need to be ever vigilant of our own needs, making sure to acknowledge and address them but keep them separate, outside of our patient encounters. We get our own needs for love, attention, adoration, and acknowledgment met elsewhere. We don't use patients as the audience for our performances or the sounding boards for our concerns. Although these parameters may seem obvious, many therapeutic relationships break down when the focus of attention gets murky and the clinician's needs begin to drive much of the clinician's behavior.

As has been mentioned several times in this book, it is acknowledged that although motivations vary, most people who enter the helping professions do so out of a strong desire to help others. Compassion and altruism are certainly noble traits, but sometimes the desire to help gets confused with the need to be needed, valued, and recognized by others for our contributions, which then has the potential to shift the relationship dynamic such that it becomes more about "us" and less about "them." The need to be needed (valued, held in high esteem) can sometimes be a corrupting force. Altruism can backfire if the clinician's need to be needed begins to distort judgment, when patient and family interactions are influenced more by the clinician's need to be respected, honored, and valued than by the patient's need for time and attention. Mindfulness, in the service of boundary awareness, serves as a helpful framework for self-reflection and self-control. Within mindfulness, we can identify our emotions and examine their influence, and look to see whether our own emotions and needs are tainting our interactions with patients.

Clinical Example 1

Jennifer Sutton is a nurse on the gynecologic oncology unit. Recent hospital budget cuts and a hiring freeze have left the unit short-staffed. Jennifer has been working extra hours in an attempt to help out during the staffing crisis but is beginning to feel exploited and exhausted. Today, Jennifer is caring for Sue Greer, who underwent a total abdominal hysterectomy 2 days ago. Sue asks "How long have you been working here?" Jennifer replies: "I've been working with GYN surgery patients here for over 10 years. In fact, last year, my expertise was recognized when I was named the hospital's Nurse of the Year. It was a really big deal. The hospital administration presented me with the award at the annual recognition dinner. " Had Jennifer taken a moment to identify her emotions and anticipate how they might make her vulnerable to nontherapeutic disclosure, she might have avoided this interpersonal shift toward self-promotion. Provided the interaction quickly refocuses back on the patient, little harm is done, but if such forays into our own ego-gratification needs become common, they can leave a patient feeling marginalized, reduced to a captive conduit through which our careers and reputations are advanced.

Mindfulness provides a framework for self-regulation, making us more conscious of the forces that lead us astray.

Had Jennifer recognized that her feelings of being under-appreciated, exploited, and frustrated by her current work situation could potentially manifest as self-serving interactions with patients, she could watch for these more carefully. She could enter Reason Mind and remember that although bragging about herself might feel good momentarily, later she would feel sullied by her obvious attempts to get her own needs met, at the patient's expense, ultimately only increasing her distress. The more mindful response to Sue's question might have taken into account that Sue may be anxious about the quality of her postoperative care. If Sue is sensing that the GYN oncology unit is short-staffed, she might also be anxious about the potential of not getting the care she needs to recover quickly. Her question to Jennifer may be an effort to determine whether Jennifer is qualified to care for her, or whether Jennifer is an inexperienced, temporary nurse brought in to fill staffing gaps. Jennifer's awareness of how short-staffing can make patients question the adequacy of their care could then be used to formulate a more therapeutic response, such as the following: "I've been working on this floor for 10 years. You sound concerned." This response provides an opportunity for Sue to speak freely and keeps the encounter patient-focused. The reply Jennifer provides is not based on memorizing therapeutic phrases; it comes naturally from a mindful assessment of potential patient needs and a willingness to conduct a brief self-assessment to determine how Emotion Mind activation, without Reason Mind scrutiny, could lead Jennifer to be much less effective in her patient encounters.

Mindfulness can also help Jennifer pull back and examine the larger system issues. She might ask herself whether it is viable for nurses to continue to be overused and over-extended because the institution is reluctant to hire more staff before being certain that the institution's census can sustain those positions. Although this is an understandable fiscal concern, the existing nurses cannot be pressured to consistently provide overtime in order to provide sufficient care. Nurses are a commodity commonly exploited when hospital budgets are tight and investment in additional personnel is considered optional.

Effective application of mindfulness is not limited to front-line professionals. A compassionate culture is cultivated when administrators collectively honor the value of system-based self-reflection. When health care systems (hospitals, agencies, practices) conduct their operations in a manner that reflects ethical boundaries, then professionals within those systems flourish. By creating a work culture where professionals are valued, respected, kindly treated, and fairly compensated, and whose time off is held sacred, administrators reflect a true commitment to the values that drive effective patient care. An institution that values its human capital and honors its social contract to provide high-quality care is also one that nurtures an atmosphere of healthy professional boundaries; it rarely asks clinicians to go "above and beyond," and when it does, it is only in times of true crisis, when *all* personnel, administrators included, are sharing the burden. Health care leaders who embrace compassion as an institutional value must extend that compassion beyond patient care and recognize that compassionate systems grow compassionate professionals and compassionate professionals provide compassionate patient care.

Health care leaders can apply principles of mindfulness to be sure that they and their institutions remain focused on promoting empathy and compassion across all levels of human interaction. Through mindfulness, administrators can monitor their own needs, feelings, drives, ambitions, and behaviors to evaluate whether they've lost sight of the core values critical to effective health care system management. Mindfulness is as important to advancing health care systems operations as it is to promoting the quality of individual patient care. Collective mindfulness can aid groups of administrators in deliberately looking within the organization's culture to detect faulty assumptions, hidden biases, or blind spots, and guide system-wide correction.

Clinical Example 2

Michael Morales is a seasoned internist. He is an avid cyclist and fly fisherman. He enjoys gourmet cooking, fine wine, and travel. Over the course of his career, he's seen substantial cuts in insurance reimbursement for his services. He practices within a multispecialty private practice group. Angelina Hernandez is a 55-year-old woman with diabetes who works on the assembly line in a commercial bakery. Although her job is tedious and uninteresting, she maintains it because of the excellent family health insurance benefits it provides. She has come into Michael's office for follow-up care for poorly controlled diabetes. She is 5 feet 3 inches tall and weighs 250 pounds. She has gained 20 pounds in the past year. Her only son died in the Iraq War 4 years ago. She lives in a trailer with her 30-year-old daughter-in-law, who is disabled, and two grandchildren. Today, her blood sugar is 220.

In an attempt to generate more revenue to make up for the insurance reimbursement shortfall, Michael has instructed the office staff to overbook his schedule. He intends to hold himself to a disciplined appointment template: 30 minutes for each new patient, 12 minutes for each follow-up case. Dr. Morales enters the exam room, agitated and harried, already 60 minutes behind schedule for the day. On their last visit, Michael spent time explaining to Mrs. Hernandez that she needed to eat more fresh fruits and vegetables, that she would have better glycemic control if she ate lean meats and/or fish several days a week, and that she needed to get regular exercise. Moreover, she absolutely had to stop eating the over-processed baked goods produced at the bakery. When looking at her current weight and blood sugar levels, Michael feels frustrated at Mrs. Hernandez's apparent lack of responsiveness to his instruction. He prides himself as being an expert in nutrition and weight loss and draws considerable satisfaction from knowing that his patients receive expert, evidence-based advice. He says: "What am I going to do with you, Mrs. Hernandez? It seems you don't want to get better. If you don't lose weight and your blood sugar continues to be high, you'll start getting problems with your peripheral circulation and you will likely lose your feet, even your legs. Then what will you do?" Certainly, the patient's blood sugar level and weight-gain problems need clinical attention, but these are not the kinds of issues that can be meaningfully addressed through time-pressured scolding. The lifestyle alterations that Michael had proposed did not take into consideration the nature and constraints of the patient's life. The recommendations were not modified to fit what is actually possible, accessible, culturally relevant, and reasonable for Mrs. Hernandez. In this current encounter, Michael is acting from a place of frustration, using his own values and insight into his own lifestyle as the context from which he is setting expectations for the patient. His Emotion Mind activation is evident in the nature of his tone, his manner, and in his word choice. The encounter is more about his need to ventilate than her need for compassionate, individualized care. One could argue that by admonishing Mrs. Hernandez for her non-compliant behaviors, Michael is actually focusing on *her* needs, but on closer inspection it is clear that his own frustration is driving his behavior. His approach is not a deliberate, skillful, compassionate attempt to help her find a way to begin to make some challenging lifestyle changes. In fact, Mrs. Hernandez is at risk for never returning to the clinic for care. Humiliation rarely motivates patients to return for follow-up.

Mindfulness

If Michael had been able to enter into mindfulness, many of the missteps in his encounter with Mrs. Hernandez could have been avoided. With mindfulness, he would have been better prepared to stop before speaking and to identify that his frustration with declining reimbursements had led him to an emotional decision to compensate by overbooking his clinic, and he might have recognized that this tight schedule set him up to experience considerable stress. He might be able to consider that such a pace could easily erode his patience and make him irritable. He also might have considered that because he prides himself in being a disciplined health advocate who works hard at maintaining his own healthy lifestyle, this predisposes him to believing that everyone else should operate from the same mindset, and that he is often quick to judge those who don't exhibit the same level of commitment to their own health and well-being. He might have remembered that, when less stressed, he does realize that his socioeconomic status allows him lifestyle advantages that are not shared by many of his patients. Having deliberately tapped into Reason Mind, he also might then have had the insight to consider that although he believes that he is not adequately reimbursed for his services, he does make a good living and is able to afford a gym membership, a lovely home, reliable transportation, and weekend cycling expeditions. He might remember that sometimes, when his time urgency and his frustration with the nation's obesity epidemic activate Emotion Mind forces, he behaves reflexively, indulging his frustrations in a manner that leaks into his patient care.

Boundaries get blurred when what he tells himself are important messages that he needs to convey to his patients become little more than thinly veiled diatribes that arise from his need to let off steam. Had his Reason Mind been deliberately solicited before he met with Mrs. Hernandez, he would have remembered that she makes minimum wage, that her son's widow is disabled, and that Mrs. Hernandez is the primary wage earner for the family. The bakery often distributes expired baked goods to the employees, giving Mrs. Hernandez access to much-appreciated free food. The family trailer is located on a rural road, far from town and shopping centers, and Mrs. Hernandez's car is reserved for necessary trips to work and medical appointments. Mrs. Hernandez has had multiple bouts of depression since her son's death. With mindfulness, the context of Mrs. Hernandez's lived experience would have been more central in Michael's consciousness and might have better informed his behaviors. Through mind*less*ness, Michael failed to honor a central tenet of boundary maintenance: Focus must be kept on the *patient's* needs.

Emotions were driving Michael's behavior. Like so many primary care physicians, Michael has dedicated his life to treating patients with chronic illness. He works in a clinic in his rural hometown and elected to do so because of a sense of commitment to the people in the community. It's his way of "giving back." But lately, he has become more aware of the salaries of his physician colleagues, especially those who went into some of the medicine subspecialties (e.g., cardiology) in the larger cities in his state. He feels cheated. Given the amount of time, dedication, and careful attention he gives his patients, and the lack of professional recognition he experiences, he is beginning to question the value of his life's work.

Michael's emotions are valid, justified, and important. They deserve attention and consideration. Michael is a thoughtful, dedicated, and compassionate professional struggling to cope with social forces that seem to denigrate his value. These are the kinds of emotions, if left unattended, that can leave professionals cynical and dissatisfied. A more mindful approach benefits both Michael and his patients. In mindfulness, he could identify and name his emotions, look at each one, and get a sense of the intensity that each one is imposing. In Body Mind, he could feel the tension, the urgency, the irritability that his body is holding. He could enter Reason Mind and see that much of his emotional distress results from his tendency to compare his work and his salary with those of his physician colleagues. When comparing salaries, he comes up short. But then he pulls back the lens and is able to observe the situation more fully. He examines broader criteria. He compares his quality of life (time with his family, time for exercise, time for friends and cooking) and he sees that much of the so-called advantages that his colleagues enjoy (e.g., money) are not as important to him as is the time he has to enjoy his life. Once reason begins to inform his emotions, he begins to experience some gratitude for the aspects of his life that he is thankful for. He then considers the gratitude that many patients frequently express to him for his thoughtful care. By shifting into Reason Mind,

Michael is able to pull up more of the facts and consider them against his strong emotions. In Wise Mind he concludes, "Well, I guess I'll never be fairly compensated for the quality of care I provide but I will enjoy my life and I do benefit from knowing that my efforts have deep meaning in the lives of people I treat." Michael's ability to use mindfulness and calm his inner storm eases his suffering and, in doing so, enhances his capacity to relieve the suffering of his patients.

Boundaries can also be violated on the opposite end of the spectrum. How often do we hear of the nurse, physician, social worker, or physical therapist who went "above and beyond" to help a patient or a family? Often these professionals are considered heroes within the community, but heroes can easily fall from grace, in part because they become vulnerable to scrutiny when their overfunctioning becomes impossible to maintain over time and they become burned out, overextended, even cynical. Their behavior can also have the unintended consequence of raising the expectations of patients and families beyond that which is reasonable to expect of a professional in the current high-paced health care system.

Clinical Example 3

Jo Ferguson is a home hospice nurse. She prides herself at being able to provide deeply comforting care to patients and families struggling with the imminent death of a loved one. Jo is experienced, personable, and technically skilled, and carries deep compassion for her patients. She is a favorite among her patients and their families. Six months ago she was written up in her local newspaper as a "regional hero." Since the article appeared, families often call the hospice for services and request Jo by name. More often than not, when she arrives at people's homes she is greeted as a local celebrity. Expectations are high.

Hospice nurses usually spend 30 to 60 minutes at each home during their daily rounds. Patients who are closer to death and whose family members are struggling to provide their loved ones with effective comfort often take more time. Jo's caseload is full. She is "on duty" every fourth to fifth weekend for urgent calls only. Yet now, since the newspaper fully described how Jo will often visit patients during her weekends off just to check in and make sure the covering nurse is doing a good job, patients now expect a higher level of care. Although Jo only provided such weekend oversight in very rare instances, she now has patients and families routinely asking for such monitoring. In fact, families are asking for Jo's home and cell telephone numbers so that they can have 24-hour access, because, as the newspaper reported, "no one is more compassionate than Jo." Not wanting to disappoint her patients and families, and certainly wanting to live up to the reputation that the newspaper has now portrayed, Jo provides the care as requested, clearly beyond what is expected by her employer, and at the cost of her personal life, her outside relationships, and her mental health. Jo will not be able to sustain such a workload long term. In fact, the very qualities that made her so effective—her nursing skill, her ability to maintain a patient-focused perspective, her sensitivity to patients' and families' thoughts, feelings, and needs— are at risk. Without properly established and maintained professional boundaries, Jo is destined for burnout.

With mindfulness, the clinician remains deeply committed to compassionate care but is better able to step back and look at the situation as an objective observer. As an observer, it is easier to note and name the emotions, motives, pressures, and expectations that are at play. In mindfulness, the clinician is better positioned to accept the uncomfortable feelings that are generated when the clinician realizes that he or she cannot be all things to all people and that for the clinician to remain effective, limits need to be applied. In accepting his or her human limitations, the clinician is freed from the bondage imposed by unrealistic expectations and is allowed to reconnect with the common humanity he or she shares with every patient the clinician serves.

Biases 9

*B*iased thinking is considered by many to be a universal human experience (Greenwald et al., 2002; Wilson,
1998). Perhaps a remnant of evolutionary survival, the
capacity to extend cooperation and compassion to one's
own group while carrying an inherent wariness toward
outsiders seems to have served our ancient ancestors well
in their efforts to sustain their respective tribes and com-
pete for limited natural resources (Wilson, 1998). But in our
fast-paced, multicultural world, these tendencies to be sus-
picious of "outsiders" can be quite problematic, especially
if such wariness is functioning at the unconscious level.
In fact, implicit negative associations are so common that
they exist concerning nearly every group in our society.

LEARNING ACTIVITY

At the Project Implicit website (www.projectim
plicit.net/index.html), numerous opportunities exist
to test our own hidden biases concerning such

(continued)

(continued)

characteristics as ethnicity, race, religion, political affiliation, gender, and body size. Online tests available on the website attempt to measure the strength of our negative biases concerning various identity traits common in our multicultural world. The purpose of these tests is not to induce guilt, but rather to illustrate just how hidden these negative associations can be and how pervasively present they are in all of us. With this heightened awareness, we can better recognize biases and make more informed decisions about whether we want to operate from them or engage in self-correction or reorientation (aka Wise Mind thinking) before acting under the influence of these negative interpersonal assumptions.

Although the health care disciplines have made much progress in identifying the importance of cultural competence in providers, most of these efforts have focused on supplying fact-based information about specific ethnic groups. Although helpful, such efforts do not go far enough to address interpersonal effectiveness. Encounters can easily be compromised if providers are responding to subtle, subliminal, and negative assumptions about patients. Such subtle negativity can easily surface without the clinician's knowledge. Because this negativity can be so difficult to detect, especially in those of us who take pride in our capacity to "treat all people the same," our devotion to the notion of "color blindness" may actually serve to further obstruct our capacity to examine the recesses of our own Emotion Mind, where these biases easily hide. Unless we accept that our human nature bestows us with innate tendencies that make us ego- and ethnocentric, we won't feel the need to deliberately examine ourselves and see what negativity might be hiding in the unexplored areas of our minds.

To promote our own objectivity, we need to regularly and systematically scan our inner experience to search for hidden biases. These detection efforts should not be considered as "search-and-destroy" missions. To the contrary, a more realistic objective is to, with a posture of humility, identify biases, then observe and describe them, without judging or criticizing ourselves. The goal is to simply detect any biases, hold them up to scrutiny, and then make more conscious decisions about if, when, or how much we want them to drive and influence our behaviors.

Although racial and ethnic differences are what people commonly think of when discussions of prejudice emerge, and are often the characteristics that are most visible, biases can exist concerning any aspect of difference. Any characteristic that sets someone apart as being different is ripe for negative association. Minor aspects of personal preference, such as hairstyles, fashion, or social group affiliation, can prompt strong negative reactions from others. For example, a patient's tattoos can trigger a clinician's implicit negative assumptions about the patient's moral character, social class, or education level. Some of the less visible sources of difference, such as political beliefs (e.g., liberal vs. conservative), lifestyles (e.g., married vs. "living together"), hobbies (e.g., NASCAR vs. art collecting), and food preferences (e.g., Southern fried vs. vegan organic), can carry within them a whole host of associated characteristics that we often assume go hand in hand with such affiliations. The list is nearly endless, but some of the more typical categories of difference that can prompt negative associations are captured in Box 9.1.

BOX 9.1 COMMON CATEGORIES OF DIFFERENCE

- Religion
- Body size
- Gender
- Sexual orientation
- Race
- Ethnicity
- Socioeconomic level
- Occupation
- Style (fashion)

- Speech (accent)
- Hygiene standards
- Foreign birth
- Education level
- Social status
- Automobile selection
- Political party affiliation

The strength of our negativity concerning any of these differences can also vary considerably. We may be quite tolerant of ethnic or racial differences but hold considerable negativity for regional affiliations. For example, a proper Southern gentleman might hold strong negativity toward those relocated New Yorkers who have "invaded" his town and who want to bring their brand of intense interpersonal confrontation to his quiet, genteel corner of the South. At the same time, the former New Yorker, now retired to this same lovely Southern city, might hold strong resentment for the native Southerners whose slow and proper manner makes "getting things done around here" so tedious.

We generalize, categorize, and sometimes demonize others in an effort to establish our identities as being in contrast to those whose ways we may find difficult to understand. With better awareness of our own hidden biases, we are better able to identify these tendencies and then to challenge ourselves to adopt a more open posture, especially if a member of the maligned group is in need of our professional care.

Clinical Example

Heather Hayes, PhD, a nurse psychotherapist, has been working in an infectious disease clinic for 6 months. In reviewing today's schedule, she sees that Walker Smith is coming in for follow-up care. Heather did a brief assessment of Mr. Smith during his previous visit to the clinic. She has some preliminary information about him: He is being treated for syphilis. He has struggled with opiate addiction for several years but has been "clean" now for 24 months. He currently lives in a group home for recovering addicts and works for a local moving company. His addiction is being treated with Suboxone. Recently, Walker has been exhibiting signs and symptoms of depression. He reports that he has a nagging sense of having wasted his life. He is 46, has two children whom he feels he barely knows, and is twice divorced. Heather works with patients who have psychiatric issues that complicate their physical care. Dr. Hayes is in the break room where staff members gather for meals and coffee. Jim Jameson, MD, the physician director of the clinic, sees her in the break room and stops in for a brief chat to review Walker's plan of care. In comparing possible treatment strategies, Heather states, "I realize that Mr. Smith's depression will put him at risk for relapse and that relapse could sabotage all of his efforts over the past 2 years, but I can't help but think that maybe his depression is inevitable. Maybe 'deadbeat dads' are just doomed for karmic retribution. He needs to make amends with his children. Until then, I don't think

I can offer him much help." Dr. Jameson, gently teasing Heather, replies, "It seems that Mr. Smith has hit a nerve with you. You are accepting of his addiction and his syphilis issues, but somehow his estrangement from his children hits a sore spot in you and has you pulling back from investing in his care." Heather is not appreciative of this feedback. She prides herself in being open-minded and nonjudgmental—how else could she effectively work with patients in an infectious disease clinic where half of the client population has HIV? Who is Jim to tell her that she "has issues"?

Blind spots are just that: areas of our thinking that manifest as tendencies that we unconsciously exhibit, that remain mostly hidden to us but that other people can sometimes detect. Heather has a negative association with Walker. His failure to actively parent his children is something that Heather finds unconscionable. Her feelings about this are strong, and they have already influenced her attitude toward the patient. She's already decided that she can't help him, and this attitude will likely be conveyed during today's session. Her preconceived opinions set her up to avoid developing rapport with Walker. Consequently, she may come across as authoritative and cold, punitive, and overbearing in her interactions with Walker. Then, when he fails to appear for their next session, she'll console herself with the notion that she was right—he wasn't going to benefit from treatment as long as his negligence toward his children remained unaddressed.

Colleagues and friends who act from a place of sincere interest and goodwill can serve as very helpful informants concerning our own negative assumptions. Their observations and thoughtful feedback can provide us with a wealth of useful information from which to expand our interpersonal effectiveness. They can detect tendencies within us that we are, oftentimes, too defensive to see. Defenses exist for a reason—they protect us from painful or anxiety-producing stimuli—but they can also sabotage our self-awareness and self-growth and act as obstacles to our compassion. Thoughtful, tactful feedback is critical to helping all of us become more effective clinicians. But too often clinicians refute feedback, avoid it, or dismiss it because it feels too threatening, too distressing. Certain feedback might create the need to reexamine our own beliefs about ourselves, our own identities, and this can feel disturbing.

But the examination of feedback need not evoke such distress. The energy we put into resisting it is often more exhausting than the energy required to accept it. Embracing feedback, with a willingness to just sit with it, look at it, and try to objectively evaluate what aspects of the feedback are true, useful, and worthy of further consideration, is an exercise in distress tolerance, of soothing Emotion Mind activation through Reason Mind scrutiny. This is the essence of mindful practice.

Acceptance is a crucial aspect of mindfulness. Acceptance of our own human nature, our own flaws and shortcomings, and our sometimes biased tendencies is a critical step. After tolerating our initial distress and displaying a willingness to accept that the feedback may have some merit, we can determine whether or not we are, at times, judgmental or condemning, or may be seen this way by others. This is especially important in situations where we are providing care.

Accepting that biased tendencies exist within all of us is not the same as operating from them. It only means that through acceptance and then scrutiny, we can deactivate such biases, we can extract from them their power to unconsciously control our behavior. Once identified, our innately human but sometimes unfounded beliefs, or "habits of mind," can be challenged and reassigned to a cognitive category of "present but often faulty notions that float around in my head."

Mindfulness allows us to heighten our awareness, to sensitize our internal radar and accept what we discover. Acceptance of difference, acceptance of biases, and acceptance of the notion that in order to avoid reflexive behaviors, it is critical to uncover, acknowledge, and scrutinize these biases, are necessary in order to avoid mindlessly operating from them. When brought into clearer view, biases can serve to remind us that we are human—that however well intentioned, we are not immune to human tendencies—and that our goal is to acknowledge and self-correct our automatic assumptions and thoughtfully choose our behaviors, with awareness.

References

Greenwald, A. G., Banaji, M. R., Rudman, L. A., Farnham, S. D., Nosek, B. A., & Mellott, D. S. (2002). A unified theory of implicit attitudes, stereotypes, self-esteem, and self-concept. *Psychological Review, 109*(1), 3–25. doi: 10.1037//0033-295x.109.1.3

Wilson, E. O. (1998). Biological basis of morality: Do we invent our moral absolutes in order to make society workable? *The Atlantic, 281,* 53–54, 56+.

Clinician Emotions   10

*T*he range of emotions experienced by clinicians spans the spectrum of human emotions in general, but certain emotions are particularly challenging for those working in health care settings. For individuals new to their respective professions, a sense of uncertainty or inadequacy, or even a fear that they might inadvertently harm someone, is typical. The sense of responsibility and accountability they feel compared to their relative lack of knowledge and experience only heightens their distress. To compensate for limited experience, newly minted clinicians sometimes exhibit a kind of hypervigilance, a compulsion to check and recheck data and review references to reassure themselves that they are being thorough and accurate. These same clinicians sometimes report a sense of feeling like an imposter, *acting* in a role rather than actually *being* a competent provider. Anxiety can be an almost constant companion for the first year or two of practice, until time and experience help them begin to feel more comfortable in their roles.

By virtue of being in the presence of pain and suffering, clinicians suffer, too. Through consistently witnessing the suffering of others, clinicians can easily absorb their patients' sadness, frustration, and even despair. Over time this can take a considerable toll. Health care providers feel the pressure of expectation when patients and families are relying on them to alleviate suffering even at times when doing so is not possible. Bodies eventually deteriorate and people die. When efforts to cure or to prolong life are no longer viable, clinicians must face the inevitability of death. This can lead to feelings of defeat, inadequacy, even futility. Defeat can also be experienced as embarrassment and even shame when clinicians have to face patients and families and admit that their efforts have failed.

Many clinical situations evoke very strong emotional reactions. Horror, grief, shock, and outrage are normal responses that many clinicians experience when faced with patients whose suffering comes as the result of violent or traumatic events. Witnessing the horrors of such injuries and the suffering that patients endure is sometimes more than clinicians can bear. Fires can leave people with unbearably painful burns that can take months of agonizing treatment to heal. Natural disasters can devastate communities, cause high numbers of casualties, and overwhelm area health care resources. Motor vehicle accidents can leave victims maimed and disfigured in ways that are truly horrifying. Intense feelings of distress cannot help but be activated in the face of overwhelming tragedy, such as when a clinician is confronted with a wailing mother who arrives at the emergency department only to learn that her 16-year-old son had died just moments before she arrived, the victim of a head-on collision caused by a drunk driver; or by the despair of a husband who learns he is dying and will leave behind his crippled wife; or when a 4-year-old dies of head injuries inflicted by her mother's angry boyfriend.

In all of these situations, clinicians are expected to carry on and to put their own feelings aside. Yet these distressing emotions persist, and without proper attention they can leave the clinician feeling vulnerable, depleted, overextended, and ultimately resentful. Life in the health care trenches can produce significant clinician casualties—providers who are deeply wounded by their exposure to unrelenting suffering. How many patients can the oncologist lose before he begins to feel as if his efforts are futile? How many depressed patients can the dialysis nurse treat before she becomes overwhelmed by her patients' despair?

Emotions are natural and justified, but there are limits to how much intense and persistent emotional activation an individual can tolerate. Over time, self-protective efforts automatically kick in and clinicians find ways of distancing themselves from the distress they feel in the face of such suffering. Again, tending to tasks rather than people is one approach to self-preservation. For example, Mr. Smith, with a fractured skull after being attacked with a baseball bat at an ATM, is reduced to being little more than "the head trauma in Room 4."

Professional boundaries serve to protect both patients and health care providers (HCPs; see Chapter 8). Boundaries keep HCPs from becoming overly involved in patient care or from making unrealistic commitments to patients and families. But sometimes, the boundaries of wounded HCPs become so inflexible that they become more like walls, and those walls grower thicker and more rigid as individuals attempt to insulate themselves from the pain of emotional investment. When clinician emotions are walled off, their compassion is walled off as well.

With one's own emotional health compromised, dealing with patients' emotions can often be experienced as just an additional burden. Tired and fatigued, some clinicians hope to call upon the psychiatry service to contend with the patients who dramatically display suffering. This can occur even in situations where the patient's emotions are quite understandable, and are no reflection of psychopathology. When patients have difficulty containing their agitated anxiety, tearful sadness, or valid frustration, they can further tax an already overburdened clinician who looks, often inappropriately, to formal psychiatric services to address these patients' needs. And although supplying a patient with additional psychosocial resources can be helpful, there is a growing tendency to pathologize a patient's emotional distress and, in doing so, shift the responsibility for addressing a patient's emotional needs to other professionals, allowing the bedside clinician to remain exclusively focused on the *purely medical* aspects of care.

Some may cite time constraints as the rationale for their detachment; this is certainly a legitimate concern, and it is true that some patients need the kind of focused distress intervention that exceeds a practitioner's skill set, but so often all that patients need is a sense that their providers have joined with them in their plight. Patients need to feel understood and accepted when their emotions spill out and their despair becomes palpable. They need clinicians who have the personal resilience to remain empathic and calm, capable of witnessing strong patient emotions without their own anxiety getting in the way. The patient needs a clinician who can remain focused on the patient's need for understanding rather than the clinician's own desire to escape the situation. Patients need physicians, nurses, social workers, and physical therapists who are able to tolerate their own distress so that the patients' distress can remain the focus of care.

Mindfulness provides a framework for mentally processing distress-provoking situations. With mindfulness, clinicians can identify the kinds of situations where patients' emotional displays of suffering are particularly distressing.

It is important to identify the emotions that are activated within us when we face these situations (fear, dread, resentment that we are being asked to respond to emotions). We can scan our own bodies for signs of emotional activation (increased heart rate, neck tension, feeling of urgency). This activation can be quite significant, and is important to note so that we can, if even for a few moments, give our full attention to it and use deep breathing or other distress-reduction techniques in order to calm down. Then we can move into Reason Mind to remember basic tenets of care, such as: "Sometimes I will experience intense emotions when faced with a patient's distress. Emotions are normal." And then move into a Wise Mind perspective: "I need to take a minute to breathe, calm down, and accept that this patient's suffering is being visibly displayed and that I have what it takes to calmly accept this. I need to honor this patient's emotions, listen, understand, and let the patient know that I will do everything I can to walk this illness journey with him and do my best to try to alleviate his suffering. It is better to tolerate some discomfort for a minute or two than to focus all of my efforts on trying to escape this situation."

Clinician emotions are not always triggered by their work. As humans, we face the inevitable pain and sorrows, losses and disappointments, stressors and relationship conflicts as everyone else. Even though when we arrive at work it would be best if we could just park our emotions at the door and enter our professional world unburdened, it is inevitable that we will carry these emotions in with us. The goal of mindful practice is not to expect ourselves to constantly transcend our own pain, but just to be aware of it, of how it might interfere with our care, and once aware of it, to take precautions. Honoring our own distress—naming it, acknowledging it, accepting that it will need to be processed and worked through—frees us from the strain of feeling as if we need to avoid or deny it. Accepting that our distress is present and that, at times, it will be knocking at our consciousness allows us to notice if it begins to seep into our interactions with patients. In mindfulness we are better prepared to notice when personal issues begin to influence professional practice. Once noticed, we can stop, retreat, rethink, rebalance, and re-enter our patient encounters, with boundaries reset, ready to try again.

Mindfulness need not add hours to the work day or interfere with the level of care provided, but it can help the harried clinician return to a sense of calm centeredness where there is space for focused attention and acceptance of all the emotions that both the clinician and patients bring. Scanning the body, identifying the emotions, taking a deep breath, and tapping into a thoughtful, detached review of the facts are crucial. Accepting that health care is difficult at times, and will inevitably evoke strong feelings, is important. Acknowledging that strong feelings are normal, valid, and important is also a key part of the process. Mindful practice helps us cultivate the resilience to tolerate our own distress, rather than feel a need to fix it or avoid it (the fight-or-flight response). Mindful practice fosters a capacity to pull back the lens, to see our ourselves and our endeavors from a broader perspective, and to remember that health care delivery is a deeply meaningful activity. Refocusing on the value of our work, on the power of compassion, and on the common humanity we share with our patients eases our suffering.

And for those clinicians in high-stakes settings such as intensive care, emergency departments, or burn units, it is even more important to cultivate mindfulness, and to seek outside sources of comfort and satisfaction. Exercise, yoga, meditation, and other mind-soothing activities are powerful antidotes to working in a stressful environment.

Note: Additional resources are listed at the end of Chapter 20.

Mistakes and Apologies

*I*n order to function effectively, clinicians need to have both confidence in their professional judgment and belief in their clinical competence. Self-assurance and poise are assets in any clinical encounter. That said, that same confidence when inflated, egocentric, or unwavering can be a significant source of diagnostic error, poor communication, and interpersonal relationship conflict. The overconfident clinician who ignores opposing evidence or overlooks additional information (often because that information calls into question the validity of his or her previously held conclusions) runs considerable risk of not only making mistakes but alienating patients and families. Damage to patient–provider relationships occurs, for example, when during an assessment or diagnostic interview, a patient's attempt to provide additional symptom information is ignored or minimized by the clinician. To the patient, it might appear that once the clinician has reached a diagnostic verdict, any additional or opposing information is dismissed. In these situations, patients sense the clinician's resistance to reconsidering the diagnostic conclusion and patients can easily interpret such resistance as the clinician's lack of interest in them or an unwillingness to engage in more thorough consideration of the patients' problems. Patients can feel discounted, misunderstood, or, even worse, ignored.

Unwavering certainty is dangerous. And it is true that it is difficult to recognize what we don't know, to realize when our thinking is biased, and to admit that our first "hunch" was wrong, but the capacity for doing so is critical (Croskerry, 2013). It is also imprudent to embrace every new idea or theory as gospel and prematurely jump on the bandwagon to endorse a new method or product solely because doing so is professionally fashionable. But a willingness to consider new information as that information becomes available, and the humility to accept that a previous conclusion was incorrect, are essential characteristics of any good clinician's problem-solving process. Otherwise, we leave ourselves prone to error and strife.

Although it is critical to clinical competence to strive toward mastery in clinical knowledge, the motives for achieving such competence can be easily obscured by blind ambition and the desire for professional recognition. It is human nature to want to excel and to experience the satisfaction that success brings, but if the motives and the emotions that fuel the drive for success are left unexamined, they can wreak havoc on our critical thinking. Hubris is a major source of mistakes within health care. And it is this hubris that also accounts for much of the downstream impact of medical mistakes. This is not the domain of physicians alone; nurses, mental health professionals, and social workers, to name a few, sometimes develop rigid mental templates on which they superimpose each patient's information. In analyzing patient information, they can easily oversimplify the process in order to accommodate preexisting hunches or quick judgments. This process can become more pronounced as clinicians gain experience. Perhaps there is no better place for humility to be regularly and deliberately activated as in diagnostic reasoning.

Patient–provider relationships are especially harmed when clinician hubris inevitably proves unwarranted, the diagnostic conclusions are erroneous, and/or mistakes occur. When a respectful, thoughtful clinician makes a mistake, patients and families may be understandably distressed—angry, frustrated, perhaps even irate—and may seek some kind of apology or restitution, but when arrogant, aloof, and dismissive clinicians make mistakes, there is a much greater likelihood that patients and families will bring formal legal action (Levinson, Roter, Mullooly, Dull, & Frankel, 1997). Without the goodwill of a well-established, mutually respectful, trusting, and positive relationship as a base, apologies can seem hollow and effective conflict resolution is unlikely.

With mindfulness, however, much of this can be avoided. With the honed practice of looking inward, we become more aware of the forces within the Emotion Mind domain that lead us away from our central goal, which is to ensure that patients receive the safest, high-quality care. With a consistent willingness to look inward, we have a better chance of establishing a kind of vigilance, looking for signs that perhaps our pursuit of clinical competence is beginning to become usurped by efforts to gain superiority and status. Or perhaps our reasoning is becoming overshadowed by the work of a trusted colleague whose recent theories seem to contrast with established practice but with whom we want to establish a professional allegiance. Or perhaps we are becoming too conflict averse, not wanting to question the clinical conclusion of a colleague because doing so might be seen as insulting. Many mistakes occur when clinicians who note a care discrepancy are too afraid to bring the problem to light, concerned that in doing so, a colleague's judgment would then be called into question and that colleague's pride compromised.

Daily surveillance helps to detect the "red flags" of hubris and bandwagon thinking so that corrective measures can be taken before self-serving motives can get a stronghold. Again, here, as in other places where our own self-interest has the potential to interfere with patient and family communication, it is important to observe this self-interest with objectivity, acknowledging it without self-criticism, but with an understanding that self-interest is human and important and necessary for survival, but problematic in places where it can interfere with our professional roles. Rather than judge or condemn our tendencies toward self-interest, we need to note when they arise in our inner experience and assess their meaning and value. Perhaps a consistent tendency toward overconfidence masks underlying self-doubt, or a sense of being unrecognized for the value of our efforts, or feelings of inferiority that we are attempting to compensate for through our work. Having needs is part of life. Meeting those needs in an effective, rather than potentially damaging, manner is a critical part of mindfulness.

Mindfulness allows for self-correction, a recalibrating of one's compassion capacity and an energy re-orientation away from ineffective self-enhancement and a refocus on patient treatment. Just as we do after taking a wrong turn on a road trip, we stop, examine the situation, adjust our thinking, and redirect our efforts back to advancing toward our desired destination, quality patient care. And in clinical practice, we find ourselves making these corrections over and over again.

Mindful clinical practice can help to both decrease the potential for mistakes and effectively address them when they happen. Being attentive, listening, doing one thing at a time, focusing, tuning out distraction, and operating from a place of humility all serve to establish compassionate relationships and promote safe and effective care. Good-will and understanding ease the tensions that come when mistakes are made and untoward, or even devastating, effects follow.

But when mistakes do happen, apologies are necessary. Apologies are best when they are sincere and delivered with humility and understanding. They are less effective when done in a rote, artificial, coerced, or defensive manner. With medical mistakes, most patients and families will want an explanation for how the mistake could have happened and/or what circumstances converged to make the mistake possible. Such explanations are less effective when it appears that the clinician or institution is trying to "make excuses." Apologies work best when clinicians enter into these difficult discussions in an environment of unhurried privacy and with a willingness to fully listen to patients and families describe their feelings about the mistake and how it has harmed them. The clinician who can tolerate his or her own distress enough to encourage those harmed to fully share their feelings and concerns, and who works hard to "seek to understand" what meaning and impact the mistake has had for them, is more effective in fostering resolution (Caplan, 2013).

Because of the legal liability issues associated with admitting fault, some providers are very reluctant to admit mistakes and accept responsibility for them. (Author's note: Because state laws may vary, it is prudent and incumbent upon clinicians to obtain competent legal advice about the implications of admitting fault, before discussing medical errors with patients and families.) Yet this admission and apology process is the action that helps to decrease malpractice claims. For that reason, 32 states have enacted laws that make apologies inadmissible in court as evidence for liability (Caplan, 2013).

An effective apology looks something like the following: "An error was made during [patient's name] care. I/we accidentally gave the wrong dose of medication. Initially her blood pressure became very low but we were able to stabilize her with other medications that counteract the blood-pressure–lowering med. She should recover fully but will need to be watched closely for the next 24 hours. I/we are very sorry that this happened. We are doing everything we can to track down how this occurred and exactly where things went wrong."

Key features of the apology include honesty, clear language that patients and families can understand, a simple but complete accounting of the incident, an estimate of the impact the error has/will have on the patient, a description of how the situation is being managed, a heartfelt apology using the words "I'm sorry," and a commitment to getting to the root cause of the error. Once the cause is known, taking responsibility is important. Some patients and families may request ongoing updates of how the institution will conduct an investigation and the mechanism the institution will use to keep them informed. This aspect should be worked out with the risk management/legal department if it occurs within an institutional setting.

References

Caplan, A. (2013). What's the right way to apologize if you've made an error? *Medscape*. Retrieved December 17, 2013, from http://www.medscape.com/viewarticle/817381

Croskerry, P. (2013). From mindless to mindful practice—cognitive bias and clinical decision making. *New England Journal of Medicine, 368*(26), 2445–2448. doi: 10.1056/Nejmp1303712

Levinson, W., Roter, D. L., Mullooly, J. P., Dull, V. T., & Frankel, R. M. (1997). Physician–patient communication. The relationship with malpractice claims among primary care physicians and surgeons. *JAMA: The Journal of the American Medical Association, 277*(7), 553–559.

Hope and Bad News

*H*ope is a universal human experience. It is the desire to fulfill a cherished dream or attain a sought-after state of being. It is a kind of optimistic longing for something that represents an improvement on current circumstances. Illness and death bring hope to the forefront of human experience. Whereas most of us delay achieving some of our life goals, caught in the illusion of having infinite time, those who are facing serious illness or approaching death can have a much keener awareness of time urgency. Hope offers an important source of comfort.

Clinicians have long recognized hope as an important contributor to patients' well-being. Instilling hope is seen as a critical function of nurses, physicians, social workers, and other health care practitioners, but sometimes clinicians struggle with how, when, and under what circumstances hope can or should be encouraged.

There are those clinicians who seem to indiscriminately encourage patients to hope for recovery and cure, without consideration of how realistic such hope may be. Other clinicians avoid discussions of hope, especially when hope for a cure is unrealistic. Still others fall prey to the trap of believing that hope is only appropriate if it is targeted toward cure alone.

Some of the confusion around hope comes from clinicians' limited view of the scope of hope. They define hope in narrow terms, seeing "cure hope" as the only meaningful kind of hope that is worth fostering. Still others wrestle with how to encourage some hope, enough to help motivate patients to adhere to treatment, without inadvertently conveying false hope, when situations do not warrant such optimism. In all of this, it is critical for clinicians to expand their perspectives, to consider a broader range of targets for hope. Hope can be channeled toward restoration of health but it can also be channeled toward more immediate goals such as an afterlife, the repair of a strained relationship, finishing an important project, or even achieving a level of insight or wisdom.

When hope for a cure (or a prolonged recovery) is realistic, then we need to encourage such hope with messages that can readily foster optimism. Communicating hope relies on choosing words deliberately in a manner that is encouraging. Although it is important to provide accurate information, this is not a time for clinicians to demonstrate their command of the scientific literature with recitations about all the results of the latest double-blind clinical trials and leave it up to the patient and family to interpret the meaning of the data or to determine the best course of treatment. Rather than saying to a patient "There is only a 23%, 5-year survival rate after aggressive treatment. It's up to you to decide how you want to proceed," consider the thoughts, feelings, and needs of the patient. The patient needs hope in order to endure the treatment and to feel it is worthwhile. The patient needs the clinician not just to report the scientific data but to make sense of those data and translate them into simple terms that patients and families can readily understand. Such discussions need to include some mention of the most likely best direction to take. Better to say: "With active treatment, you have a good chance of surviving this episode of the illness. Such treatment will be uncomfortable at times, but will allow you to maintain much of your current lifestyle." This is a time when word choice and clinician demeanor are acutely meaningful to the patient. It is far more comforting for a patient to hear "With the new drugs now available, the tumor can shrink and you can go into long-term remission, living several more years of productive life," than to be told something like "We cannot cure it; we can only shrink the tumor temporarily. It will grow back and eventually our drugs won't be effective anymore." Yes, patients may want more precise prognostic information, but often their questions evolve over time and more information can be provided gently, thoughtfully, and sensitively during subsequent encounters as the clinical context unfolds and circumstances warrant. Patients and families need time to process information and rally support. This is easier if challenges can be presented to them gradually, sequentially, and with resources offered to them at each phase. When the patient's prognosis is terminal but death is months or years away, such news is often best conveyed in a gradual and gentle manner, but it still needs to be accurate and truthful. Tact is not the same as deception. If news is to be delivered in installments, then it is critical that all installments are provided, so that the patient does not receive partial, misleading, or incomplete information. Again, mindfulness is important. The clinician or team of clinicians must have a formal plan for conveying essential information so that, over time, the patient has a full understanding of the situation and can make plans accordingly.

However, when hope is channeled primarily into hope for a cure, when cure is not realistic, this undermines trust in the patient–provider relationship. Clinicians who promote unrealistic cure hope deceive patients, and sometimes themselves.

Fear of dying is part of the human experience. That fear manifests not only in those patients experiencing terminal illness, but in the health care providers caring for them. Anxiety about death fuels patients' and clinicians' desire for the situation to be different. Clinicians too want to be able to hope that the patient will survive, even when the clinical situation suggests otherwise. And although this might seem noble on the surface, it may be an unconscious attempt to soothe ourselves, to calm our own anxieties about the limits of health care and the finite nature of life. If false hope is encouraged, in part, in order to meet clinicians' need to dissipate their own anxiety, it becomes self-serving and could even represent a boundary cross-over phenomenon whereby the motivation for a clinical decision becomes primarily self-serving.

Providing false hope may also be motivated by expediency. It is much easier, quicker, and less anxiety provoking to provide false reassurances and platitudes about continuing to "fight" than to help patients address emotion-laden feelings of distress that surround death. These perspectives on instilling false hope are not provided to induce guilt or pass judgment, only to shed light on common, often habitual, ways in which clinicians interact with patients without considering downstream impacts or unintended consequences. Mindful interaction compels us to shine the light of scrutiny onto our often unexamined assumptions, question their accuracy, and consider alternate approaches. The commonly held assumption that instilling hope for a cure is a universally helpful gesture requires considerable examination. Yes, hope can lift one's spirits and focus energy toward a desired outcome, but it needs to be honored as a valuable force that is channeled in an honest direction.

Hope can also provide comfort when it is directed toward important, non–cure-related targets—hope for an afterlife, to die pain free, to live until a cherished loved one is able to come visit, or to live until a grandchild is born. Hope can be cultivated around reconciliation, forgiveness, and under-standing within important relationships. Hope can be gener-ated around achieving a sense of having lived a meaningful life and leaving an important legacy. Patients often hope that they will peacefully move through the transition to death and that their loved ones will have the support and perspec-tive needed to cope with their absence. In all these "hopes" there is the opportunity for the patient to do considerable work—engage in difficult conversations, write letters, finish projects, consult resources, and provide direction. Beyond just getting their affairs in order, when patients are given hon-est information with realistic expectations, they are free to move through the final phase of psychosocial development, to engage in a search for meaning, to consider their life's successes and failures, and to put these in perspective in a way that allows them to achieve peace as they move toward any reconciliation efforts that need their attention. They may even have the opportunity to achieve a sense of ego integrity (Erikson, 1950), even wisdom. Clinicians inadvertently rob patients of such opportunities when they cling to false hope for a cure and instill that false hope in their patients, because by doing so clinicians focus patients' attention away from the work of dying and encourage patients to channel their dwindling energy into a futile fight for life.

To encourage noncure hope requires clinicians to move into their own state of mindful acceptance of death. Although this is initially painful for clincians, as it is for their patients, it is the next step in the sequence of providing compassionate, patient-centered care. By accepting the terminal phase of a patient's illness, the clinician takes on a demeanor of calm resolution that serves the clinician well as the patient expresses the inevitable emotions he or she faces when death becomes real. With this equanimity, the clinician is in a much better place to listen, support, validate, encourage, and extend compassion as the patient moves through the critical phases of coming to grips with his or her fate. The following scenario illustrates an example where the nurse is likely to experience considerable anxiety. Nurses often deflect such discussions to physicians, even though they may be very aware of the patient's actual clinical situation. To be fully honest and authentic means to not be compelled to escape from such discussions because of anxiety or fear of "saying the wrong thing." An example of effective interaction is as follows:

Patient: I've felt so awful lately and I know that the chemotherapy isn't working the way we'd hoped. Am I going to die?

Nurse: What has your physician told you about this?

Patient: She said that if this chemo didn't work, there were few other options.

Nurse: So your understanding is that if this chemo isn't effective, it's unlikely that you will recover from your cancer?

Patient: Yes, that's right.

Nurse: I'm sorry. Of course you'd be upset about that. [Pause here, leaving time for the patient to process your words.] Well, assuming that your understanding is accurate, what most concerns you right now?

Patient: My biggest concern is that I'm going to die. I'm not ready to die; I can't imagine leaving my family and never seeing them again.

Nurse: Thoughts about death can be really scary, and feelings of sadness and loss are understandable. I'm so sorry.

Patient: I've been worried about this all along. I knew the cancer was bad but I didn't think it would be so aggressive.

Nurse: Yes, it can be a particularly aggressive kind of cancer.

Patient: How long do you think I've got?

Nurse: I don't know. This is a good question for your oncologist. I can put a call into him to see when he might be coming by.

Patient: [crying] What happens after we die? Do you think there really is a heaven or some kind of afterlife?

Nurse: I think that different people have different ideas about this. What do you think? Do you have a faith or religion that helps you think about such questions, one that you've called upon to help you get through difficult times?

Patient: I believe that there is life after death, and that I've lived a good life, so I don't worry about 'getting in' to heaven. I'm just not ready to leave yet. What will happen to my husband? He'll need help.

Nurse: I understand. There is a lot to think about. [Provide a few moments of silence here to allow the patient time to be with her feelings and for you to just be with her, in those feelings.] Well I think there are a few things that might help you. First, have a candid conversation with your physician about treatment options and what you can expect. You need to be sure that you have the most accurate information. Next, if what you suspect is true, consider what resources you want to draw from for help and support for both you and your husband. We have people here who can assist you. We have chaplains, social workers, and even a specially trained nurse who helps patients talk about these kinds of issues.

The nurse then provides several more nuanced sources of hope: hope that the patient will not suffer alone—that others are available to listen, understand, and offer support; hope that she will have resources available to help her address spiritual issues; hope that there is assistance available, for herself and for her husband as well.

In this scenario, the nurse is being asked some very tough questions. He is faced with an emotional patient grappling with what are perhaps the most painful moments of her life. The nurse is being asked questions that he cannot answer yet are important for him to respond to. More valuable than any other technique in his communication skill set is his capacity to be mindful, to acknowledge how easy it is for these types of discussions to activate his Emotion Mind domain. If he were to operate from Emotion Mind alone, he'd likely be blind to his escalating anxiety and simply respond to the patient's initial question of "Am I going to die?" with a stereotypical "No need to talk about dying. You don't know what will happen. It's important to wait and see and keep up a fighting spirit." Such a response might serve the immediate need of decreasing the nurse's anxiety and temporarily pacifying the patient, but more likely the patient will take away the message that this nurse doesn't want to talk about such painful topics and the patient will be left to suffer through her fear and doubt on her own. With a commitment to mindfulness and deliberately shifting into the Reason Mind domain, the nurse is able to identify that end-of-life conversations are a critical part of health care delivery. Within the Wise Mind domain, he can reflect on the finite nature of life, on the inevitability of death, on the value of helping patients peacefully move through this final transition, on the need to channel hope into honest, constructive directions that enhance patient and family experiences. He can acknowledge that his own Emotion Mind thinking will be activated when patients bring up end-of-life issues and that he will need to consistently identify his Emotion Mind thinking, scan his body to recognize the muscle tension and stomach tightening he feels, and deliberately shift to Reason Mind considerations such as "death is very anxiety producing in patients and clinicians alike, and I will feel uncomfortable when in these situations." He then needs to shift to a Wise Mind orientation, where he can access ideas such as these: "This is tough and I feel badly for this patient, but in the long run she will do better if I can tolerate my own anxiety, provide her with compassion, listen, attend to her needs, validate her feelings, and eventually provide resources, rather than jump into simply trying to temporarily soothe her fears."

When clinicians can accept their own discomfort and yet strive to be present with the distressed patient, they allow for the kind of deep human connection that provides the patient with an opportunity to express deeply held fears that can be difficult to share with family members and that, if left unspoken, can leave patients to suffer alone. Instilling hope means asking questions such as these:

1. In the time you have left, what kinds of things do you want to accomplish?
2. Is there someone you would like to talk with, someone with whom you've had difficulty and would like to work with to repair the relationship?
3. Are there plans or arrangements to make or projects to finish while you have time to attend to them?
4. Are there people you'd like to contact in order to clarify an issue or help you with a problem?
5. What do you need help with, and who do you want to have assist you in developing a plan for getting that help?

Some patients also do well when they have an opportunity to make meaning from their lives, to reminisce and to put in perspective their life's struggles and accomplishments. Asking prompting questions and being willing to listen to their replies can help patients move through this process. Questions such as the following are appropriate:

1. How do you want to be remembered by your friends and loved ones, and is there anything you'd like to do now to help them remember you?
2. For what are you most proud of in your life?
3. Looking back at all the challenges, obstacles, hardships, successes, and triumphs in your life, what stands out?
4. As you look back over your life, what lessons have you learned that have most surprised you?
5. Who and what have meant the most to you?

These are just general leads that help patients begin the process of getting their affairs in order—sharing important words with loved ones, putting into perspective the joys and challenges of their lives, and transitioning to death. With the help and acceptance of a mindful clinician, the patient can experience a sense of being heard, understood, and valued as a whole person. Mindful clinicians can approach such encounters with a willingness to embrace difficult discussions, confident that doing so is another important aspect of compassionate care.

Reference

Erikson, E. (1963). *Childhood and society* (2nd ed.). New York, NY: Norton.

Grief

Grief is an inevitable part of life. We grieve our own personal losses and at times we grieve for the deaths of
patients we have encountered through our work. We witness the grief of patients' loved ones and are often called to
offer comfort and support. As health care providers, we are
expected to effectively deal with our own grief so that we
don't become overwhelmed by it, and so that we can remain
emotionally available to patients and families. This emotional
availability requires of us the capacity to move through our
own periods of mourning in a manner that is thoughtful and
constructive, and yet rarely are we taught how to do this.
Mindfulness provides some useful principles.

Deliberate self-assessment is the first step. Acknowledging
our losses and considering their meaning help to leave us
more open to further our self-understanding. Mining our
inner experience for both obvious and more subtle emotions helps us uncover hidden feelings. Bringing these feelings forward to be examined in Reason Mind, where they
can be viewed from multiple perspectives, made sense of,
and processed, is the next step. In Reason Mind, we bring
in facts to consider and place our emotions in context.

Wise Mind allows us to appreciate our experiences, accept our vulnerabilities, and move back into the patient care arena with a sense of renewed capacity for shifting our focus outward again.

Lindsey Moore is a seasoned oncology nurse. She works as a nurse navigator with patients diagnosed with breast cancer. In her role, she manages a large caseload of patients and oversees the coordination of their care across medical-oncology, surgical-oncology, radiation-oncology, and other services. Recently, several of her long-term patients have entered the end-stage disease phase of their illness. Lindsey has known many of these women for 5 years or longer. Through her work she has come to know their partners, their children, and some of their siblings. She is considered by many of them to be a critically important part of their illness experience. Two of her favorite patients died in the past month. For one of those patients, she gave the eulogy at the patient's memorial service.

In the past week, Lindsey has found herself tearful and apprehensive during her morning drive to work. She is short-tempered with colleagues, demanding of lab personnel, and emotionally distant with her immediate supervisor. She is counting the days until her 2-week vacation but the departure date is still months away. She avoids returning patient phone calls, then finds herself stuck late at her office, trying to catch up. She's been saying things to her husband like "What's it all for? All this work and effort and energy and they just die anyway! I thought I would be working on a team that saved lives, but it seems like all we do now is attend funerals."

Lindsey is tired, overwhelmed, and no longer able to maintain a balanced perspective. She is lost in her emotions and struggling to make sense of her experience. Her distress is leaking out into her work but she's not consciously aware that her attitude is serving only to aggravate the situation. Her suffering is palpable but her insight is obscured.

Were Lindsey to move into a state of mindfulness, she might be able to begin to "unpack" her distress. The connection between her change in demeanor and the deaths of two important patients might be more obvious to her. Her grief, her anger, her sense of disappointment, and her frustration would be more accessible. Having identified these, she might be able to see that each one of these emotions is valid, a natural part of grieving. She could talk about these feelings with her supervisor or her husband and unload some of the strain she is experiencing by holding these emotions inside. With a body scan, she might be able to sense where she is holding her grief and how it is manifesting itself physically. She might also then see the value in relaxing in a manner that is soothing, perhaps through walking, yoga, or taking a bath. Accessing Reason Mind might allow her to think clearly about the stages of grief, the nature of loss, and the typical feelings that grief evokes. And, eventually, when she is able to enter Wise Mind, she can reconsider the perspective that she cannot keep patients alive, but she can add significantly to their quality of life and help immeasurably as they transition to death.

Expressing Condolences 14

Sometimes when our patients die, we, as health care providers, struggle with when to, how to, and to whom we should express our sympathies. In many cases we express those condolences verbally at the bedside at the time of death, or perhaps later through a follow-up phone call. For some patients with whom we have worked closely or been significantly involved, we might choose to send survivors a formal condolence note. For the patient's loved ones it is especially comforting to receive notes of sympathy from closely involved clinicians (Kane, 2007). But before setting pen to paper, many factors might need to be considered (see Chapter 13: Grief).

Taking a few moments for quiet reflection to tap into our own inner experience and measure our internal climatic conditions is the first step when bringing a mindfulness-based approach to this effort. Some useful questions to prompt the assessment include these: When thinking about the deceased, what Emotion Mind messages are being generated? Is there a sense of deep sadness or frustration that the patient could not have been saved or cured? Is there a sense of despair that our efforts to help seemed futile or inadequate? Is there an aspect to this patient's struggle with his or her specific illness or trauma that generates within us a sense of injustice? Then we must ask ourselves: How is the body holding these emotions? Scanning the body for muscle tension, gastrointestinal distress, and sensations of pressure or pain can provide additional data that tell us we are carrying our distress in very physical ways. Being able to identify these feelings and sensations is useful in bringing them to the forefront of consciousness. Once identified, emotions can be examined more closely. They can be verbalized, shared with a trusted friend or colleague, discussed, and processed. By examining and processing our emotions, we become far more aware of their presence and influence. We can then monitor how, when, and to whom we express them, being particularly careful to control how we share them with the deceased's loved ones. This is important because the primary purpose of extending condolences is to comfort those who are intimately connected to the deceased rather than in some way trying to discharge our own pain or suffering (Silk & Goldman, 2013).

With an ongoing commitment to mindful practice, we can more easily acknowledge the distress we feel when patients die. Using principles of mindfulness, we can deliberately take time to look inward, note and identify emotions, and accept the depth and intensity of our feelings. In doing so, we become better positioned to manage our distress effectively. Then, when responding to the bereaved, we are able to operate more objectively, focused on them rather than on ourselves.

With mindfulness, we recognize that condolences need to be stated with extra sensitivity. With our own feelings identified, processed, and managed, we can respond to the needs of the bereaved, with consciously selected, helpful messages, conveyed in a manner that is designed solely with their needs in mind. If we are only partially aware of our own emotions, we run the risk of responding to others in a manner that may actually serve to soothe ourselves. We might inadvertently unload our own angst, rather than offer thoughts that comfort the patient's loved ones.

Once in the right mindset, we can then move into writing an expression of our sympathies. Basic components of offers of condolence include:

- Expressions of sorrow, such as: "I am so sorry for your loss. I am saddened by the death of your mother."
- A description, anecdote, or fond memory of the deceased, recounted in a warm and gentle manner, so as to be especially meaningful to survivors. Examples include:
  - "She had an innate cheerfulness that I really admired."
  - "I will miss her stories about her wonderful experiences while traveling abroad."
  - "I was so impressed by his steadfast commitment to his family."
- A wish for comfort, such as: "My heartfelt condolences to you and your loved ones during this difficult time."

Although many clinicians may consider mentioning the deceased's "long, hard and courageous struggle with [cancer, dementia, cystic fibrosis, etc.]," sometimes these notions are controversial, especially the reference to "courage," and can seem somewhat cliché. It is better to focus on a specific noteworthy feature of the deceased's personality in order to individualize the expressed sentiments.

Usually, the most effective condolence notes are ones that reflect the three components mentioned earlier, are relatively brief, and are constructed with the sole purpose of providing comfort and support to the bereaved.

References

Kane, G. C. (2007). A dying art? The doctor's letter of condolence. *CHEST Journal, 131*(4), 1245–1247.

Silk, S., & Goldman, B. (2013, April 7). How not to say the wrong thing. *The Los Angeles Times.* Retrieved from http://articles. latimes.com/2013/apr/07/opinion/la-oe-0407-silk-ring-theory-20130407

Disgust   15

*D*isgust may seem like an odd topic to highlight in a book dedicated to enhancing patient–provider relationships, but it bears special consideration given that it is rarely openly discussed even though it is a common phenomenon. In the course of our work, clinicians are exposed to patients' most basic human products: urine, feces, pus, blood, and vomit, to name a few. We see gaping wounds, disfiguring traumas, and exposed bones. These are aspects of life that your average banker, engineer, or construction worker would rarely experience in a day on the job. We encounter smells, see anatomical parts, hear bodily sounds, and touch things that people outside of health care can only imagine. Some of these things are very difficult to experience, and yet doing so is not only part of the job, but doing so *graciously, with acceptance and sensitivity*, is a gesture of compassion. Being in a state of mind to make that compassion happen is aided by mindfulness. Consider the following example:

Ms. Bridget Thompson is a 45-year-old woman admitted to the local hospice with end-stage pancreatic cancer. Yvonne Martin, her nurse, is trying to provide supportive, respectful palliative care and enhance Bridget's sense of being able to die with dignity. Fifteen years ago Bridget had a significant rectal tear during the delivery of her second child, which left her with compromised rectal sphincter control. Now, she is having episodes of fecal incontinence with significant amounts of foul-smelling diarrhea. Yvonne, and the nursing assistant, Maggie, are struggling to keep Bridget clean and dry. Bridget is embarrassed, horrified actually, by her incontinence and her shame is contributing to her agitation and anxiety. She, herself, is nauseated by the diarrhea. She can't imagine how difficult it must be for Yvonne and Maggie.

Bridget: [in tears] This is so awful. Dying like this is so humiliating. Why can't God just take me now so all of us can stop having to deal with this mess! It's repulsive!

Yvonne: [softly, slowly, calmly] I know you are upset about it, but the diarrhea should subside soon. We've given you some medications that should work to stop it. In the meantime, we will get through this together. Maggie and I know that this is just another symptom of the illness. It's not a reflection of you, your value, or your hygiene. We are okay.

The acceptance that Yvonne extends to Bridget is gracious, sensitive, and affirming. This expression of calm kindness is a true gesture of compassion. Yvonne makes clear to Bridget that the diarrhea is *not* Bridget, or a reflection of Bridget's character or value; it is merely a product of the illness. Such gracious acceptance allows Bridget to create emotional distance between her and the diarrhea rather than feeling like it is a part of her or that it defines her.

Externalizing the unpleasant phenomenon and perceiving it as something outside the patient, outside the patient's control, is helpful to Yvonne as well and critical to effective interactions. Had Yvonne or Maggie become lost in their own suffering, with their respective internal dialogs deteriorating into something like "I can't believe this! How disgusting. I'm probably going to gag. I didn't sign up for this! Get me out of here," then everyone's suffering would have been amplified and a critical opportunity to extend the healing power of compassion would have been missed.

For clinicians, staying focused on the essence of the patient, the patient's personhood, rather than the unpleasant excrement, wound, or tissue, and shifting attention to that personhood is valuable to both patient and practitioner. Focusing on the patient, stepping into her shoes, and feeling what it must be like for Bridget allow Yvonne and Maggie to transcend the olfactory stimulus and bring focused attention to Bridget's suffering, her need for affirmation and dignity. Their efforts to focus on relieving Bridget's suffering support the goal of Bridget being able to die with dignity. Yvonne and Maggie, mindful of their power to heal Bridget's suffering, experience a kind of transcendence that allows them to connect with the common humanity within us all.

Difficult Encounters   16

*O*ften, clinicians carry subconscious expectations of patients and patient behaviors. The range of expectations can be broad, but individual expectations can also be subtle. We can believe that patients *should* be cooperative, clean, cordial, appreciative, polite, compliant, cheerful, and always punctual. They *should* be full participants in their care, and come from supportive and loving families who are readily available and have adequate resources. They *should* value our efforts and hold us in high esteem. They *should* be attractive and intelligent while they eat right, don't smoke, stay fit, and get 8 hours of sleep each night. They *should* respond to treatment, recover completely, and lead long, productive, healthy, and stress-free lives. They *should* be and do these things, but more times than not, they aren't and don't.

These statements are certainly oversimplified representations of our subconscious thinking, but sometimes our hidden assumptions about how things or patients *ought* to be strongly influence our reactions when the reality is something different. The *shoulds* get in our way. These subtle expectations can act as a set of entitlements that, when violated by a patient or family, can impose a barrier to our being able to provide effective care. Even more challenging is when it seems as if the patient is deliberately interfering with our treatment. In trying to understand a patient's behavior, we get caught in our assumption that whatever it is that the patient is doing should not be happening. How can we bring mindfulness into difficult encounters?

Clinical Example

Megan Atwater is a 30-year-old woman with cystic fibrosis and bilateral lower lobe pneumonia. This is her third hospitalization for pneumonia in 6 months. Her nurse, Caitlyn, comes into Megan's room with her antibiotic. Megan refuses to take the medication, saying that she has tried it before and it hasn't worked. She explains that she has come to this hospital, far from home, because it is the regional center for cystic fibrosis treatment and she expected to receive more innovative care. If she were going to be given the same medication she'd tried as an outpatient at home, she never would have agreed to come. Caitlyn, because of having to tend to the needs of another, acutely ill, patient, is behind schedule in giving morning meds. She suggests to Megan (with a slightly impatient manner) that Megan should just take the med for now and then later discuss her concerns with the medical team members when they make rounds. Megan is not persuaded. With an angry edge to her voice, she replies "You can take that medication out of here and go tell the team yourself!" Caitlyn walks away mumbling under her breath "Who does she think she is; she's so rude." Caitlyn phones Travis, the intern, and explains the situation, emphasizing the patient's unpleasant and demanding behavior. Travis comes up to the floor to intervene. He enters Megan's room, saying, "Megan, I understand that you are not happy with our choice of medication for you. I don't think you understand that according to several randomized, controlled clinical trials with cystic fibrosis patients, this antibiotic was proven to be quite superior to . . . ." Megan interrupts him, "Look, I don't care about your studies; I've tried it before. It didn't work. I didn't come all this way to be given a treatment I could have been given by my doctor at home!" Travis, getting annoyed, says, "Megan, it might not have worked then, but you don't know that it won't work now. I did a lot of research before deciding on this med. It took me a long time to review all the literature and select this one. I'll be presenting your case to the team this afternoon and it would be good for all of us if you could cooperate with your treatment." Megan responds angrily, "Good for all of us! What do you mean? This isn't about you! It's my treatment—it's my life at stake!"

Neither Caitlyn nor Travis has addressed Megan's concerns. They are distracted by the emotions that Megan's behavior is triggering in them.

Their Emotion Mind activation is strong and their Reason Mind thinking is focused solely on persuading Megan to take the medication rather than on understanding her thoughts, feelings, and needs. Both Caitlyn and Travis are offended by Megan's brusque, angry manner. They had expected Megan to be cooperative, compliant, understanding, and maybe even appreciative of their efforts. After all, they are sincerely trying to be helpful in treating her illness. But instead, she seems to them to be impatient, demanding, entitled, and resentful. What is difficult for Caitlyn and Travis to see is that they are so focused on treating Megan's illness (while being caught up in their emotions) that they've lost track of the need to treat Megan the person. They've not assessed Megan's thoughts, feelings, and needs. They have been *goal focused* rather than *patient focused*.

Travis's attending physician, Amy Worthington, is walking by the room and hears Travis trying to talk Megan into taking the medication. Amy walks in, warmly introduces herself, and asks if she could be of help. The following dialog then takes place:

Megan: I don't want one more person trying to shove this medication down my throat.

Amy: [calmly and slowly] I don't blame you. If I were you, I wouldn't want that either. You feel like we are trying to force it on you.

[Megan then describes her refusal to take the medication and her anger at the team for pushing something on her that she knows won't work.]

Amy: Well it sounds like you have some good experience in monitoring your illness. How do you see us as being most helpful to you?

[This open-ended question taps into Megan's broader concerns.]

Megan: You can help me survive.

Amy: You sound worried.

[With this approach, Megan's demeanor changes. She begins to open up, with sadness mixed with anger in her voice.]

Megan: This is my third bout of pneumonia in 6 months. We all know what that means—I'm reaching the final stage of my illness. If I can't recover soon, my only option will be lung transplant. Lung transplantation is hell, and we all know it.

Amy: Tell me what you understand about lung transplantation.

Megan: I've done my homework on this. Only 50% of people survive 5 years, and those 5 years are often filled with problems like rejection and infections. I don't want to go through that, and I can't stand the idea of putting my family through it. My daughter is only 5. I don't want her to remember me as a sickly mother whose medical costs bankrupted the family and left her motherless in the end anyway.

Amy: So you have put your faith and hope in us. You are counting on us to be able to come up with a treatment that treats your pneumonia and helps to get you back home to your family. I can see that there's a lot at stake here.

Megan: You bet there is. And that stupid medication is not going to get me well.

Amy: I see your point. Well, one thing is clear: I think we all have the same ultimate goal, and that is to successfully treat your pneumonia and get you back home. We will do everything we can to address the pneumonia and help you avoid the need for a transplant. It would help if you could give us a list of the treatments you've tried over the past year and which ones have been helpful. Also, give us a few hours to meet with the team and some of our consultants and put together some ideas for a plan. Then we can run those by you and see what you think. We really want to work together on this. Sound okay?

Given Megan's diagnoses, and her age, Amy had suspected that Megan's lungs might be failing and that transplant could be on the horizon. Amy is aware that transplant is a very stressful experience for patients and families. Amy also knows that patients are agitated and irritable when afraid and that they can feel isolated and alone when hospitalized. She had all this information in her mind before she met Megan. She also knew from overhearing the patient's interaction with the intern that Megan was angry, disappointed, and questioning the appropriateness of her care. Amy thought that she herself might respond the same way if she ever found herself in Megan's shoes. Just before entering the room, Amy was able to adjust her inner climate, knowing she was going to walk in on an angry altercation, but she was already prepared to see the patient's emotions in context, not as a reflection of her own worth or value, but more as a reflection of the patient's inner turmoil. Because Amy didn't have to process any reactive inner emotions, she was able to bring her full attention to the patient with a desire to understand and a willingness to listen even if the patient's feelings might be expressed in an angry and accusatory way. With a focus on the patient's thoughts, feelings, and needs, Amy was able to explore the situation from a broader frame of reference. She took the time to explore a little more of Megan's situation and validate Megan's feelings. She also deliberately brought Megan in as a full participant in her own care, rather than treating Megan as an object of treatment. She joined with, rather than opposed, Megan around a common goal and placed herself on Megan's team—all without any hint of taking on an air of superiority. In a very short time, Amy was able to attend to Megan the person, provide comfort and compassion, and move Megan's treatment forward, out of the stalemate that had been evident only minutes before.

When working with a patient who seems to sabotage his or her own care, or who questions our every recommendation, or who even insults our expertise, our emotions can be strongly activated. And although natural and understandable, these emotions, left unprocessed, often serve to obstruct rather than enhance our capacity to function smoothly. When patients behave in a manner that is outside the implicitly expected "standard," our emotions are activated. From those emotions come judgments, usually negative judgments, that categorize patients and provoke a set of responses. Those responses can seem to come from a set of covert operations, a strategy to regain dominance on the playing field, sometimes head on, sometimes through a kind of oblique defensive action. Although dealing with difficult patients certainly requires thoughtful strategizing with tact and grace, dominance is not usually effective.

The mindfulness skills that Amy portrayed were well established. She was able to experience the patient without judgment or reactivity. Her negative emotions were not activated by Megan's anger or rudeness. Amy was able to stay fully present, in the moment, giving Megan her full, complete attention with an attitude of wanting to understand. Amy was able to distance herself from a sense of needing to immediately fix something. She didn't take on Megan's distress or urgency; she just worked to understand it. She simply accepted Megan's feelings and behaviors as they were, without any sense that Megan should be behaving differently.

Mindfulness practice provides the clinician with a set of principles for reconsidering the "should." In mindfulness, the angry, nonadhering, resistant patient is considered just as he or she is: a product of genetics, environment, and life circumstances that converge to create the difficult person before us—neither good nor bad, right nor wrong.

There are some situations in which all patient-centered efforts fail to achieved a workable relationship with a patient and family. In these cases, it is important for clinicians to convey clear expectations and limits and convey them consistently across disciplines. The purpose of limit setting is never so that clinicians can assume a position of power, or as a means of punishing patients. Limits are constructed for the sole purpose of establishing clear expectations for both patients and providers. Some of this was discussed in Chapter 8: Boundaries.

Somatic Complaints

When patients exhibit symptoms that seem exaggerated or feigned, clinicians often bristle, exhibiting frustration, even contempt. Compassionate providers easily rally around sick children, innocent and helpless, who need us and to whom we can offer profound comfort. Sick children tap into our deepest wells of empathy. Patients whose symptoms are suspected of being overstated, dramatized, or serving to achieve some kind of secondary gain are often reviled by those assigned to their care. It's okay for a clinician's heartstrings to be tugged by a case of an innocent and helpless victim, but if those heartstrings are being tugged deliberately, in an effort to gain some kind of privilege or unearned advantage, clinicians feel deceived, duped, and angry. There is a sense of being exploited, taken advantage of, even made a fool of by those patients who "manipulate" clinicians and abuse the health care system. Compassion evaporates and is often replaced by contempt.

Clinicians' thinking in these cases can become easily polarized. Somehow, with even the suggestion that a patient's symptoms might be unfounded, clinicians' sentiments can take an abrupt turn from empathy to scorn. Yet only in rare cases do patients actually feign illness. More often, complex biopsychosocial interactions are at play where patients' fears, anxieties, and subtle, often unconscious motives come together to significantly impact their illness experience. This is neither deliberate nor nefarious.

Stress, in its many complex and idiosyncratic forms, wreaks havoc on health. Illness and trauma are inherently stressful. When a trauma victim enters the emergency department covered in blood and with gaping wounds, some of the patient's distress is likely to be from the pain of the injuries and some is likely to be from fear of the experience. There is no way to determine how much each source of agony is contributing to the patient's distress. Nor is it useful to consider that only the distress that is generated from the physical trauma is worthy of attention, that the emotional trauma is separate and needs to be considered suspect. The two are inextricably tied together. So it is with most maladies. The degree to which any condition or ailment is exacerbated by the emotions of its host is varied and impossible to objectively measure.

Who among us has not struggled to decide whether or not to call in sick on a day when a nasty cold has left us listless, coughing, and uncomfortable but maybe not quite compromised enough to stay home? Was our condition bad enough to warrant a day of hot tea, TV, and being waited on by our loved ones, or were we just feeling sorry for ourselves, succumbing to a desire for a day off to indulge in rest and recovery, excused from our normal duties and responsibilities? How do we determine what constitutes symptoms that are "bad enough" to warrant clinical consideration, much less special attention? Can we be entirely objective and can our motives be entirely pure? No.

From the high school student who takes advantage of a headache to leave school just before the dreaded calculus exam to the exhausted assembly-line worker whose arthritis pain makes it possible for her to qualify for "workplace accommodation" and a deeply desired desk job, examples of potentially compromised motives abound. Unfortunately, there are no methods for clearly distinguishing between symptoms that are entirely organic and those that are influenced by emotional needs for comfort, relief, and attention. We all suffer, some of us more than others, but to assume that another's expression of illness is motivated primarily by a desire to shirk responsibility, fool clinicians, or obtain unearned advantage reduces complex human phenomena to simple acts of deliberate deception. Illness is a complex experience with all manner of cultural, psychological, social, and environmental aspects.

Clinical Example

Marsha Edwards is a 22-year-old woman who was 20 weeks pregnant at the time of admission to the perinatal inpatient unit because of protracted vomiting, weight loss, and dehydration. Three weeks into her stay, the nurses and physicians began to question the validity of her reports. Well into the second trimester of her pregnancy, they questioned the accuracy of her nausea and wondered whether her vomiting was, at least in part, self-induced. At times, she appeared content to be taken care of in a lovely hospital room, surrounded by her parents and friends. Her employer's generous sick-leave benefits allowed her to draw a full salary while hospitalized. Her mother doted on her, heavily invested in contributing to the term birth of a healthy first grandchild. The team suspected that Marsha was exaggerating her distress, and in doing so, was bilking the system out of thousands of mis-spent health care dollars that should have been targeted to patients who are actually sick. Several of the obstetrics residents explored the possibility of installing hidden cameras in the patient's room in an effort to catch her at gagging herself into a vomiting episode. When clinician interactions with Marsha took on an accusatory, adversarial, and dismissive tone and Marsha and her parents began to sense, and resent, the contempt, tempers flared. When Marsha's father, a blue-collar worker whose guarded demeanor and gruff manner had already tainted staff opinion, strongly voiced his complaints, he was labeled as disruptive and security was called to escort him from the hospital.

The clinicians believed that they were being duped, made fools of, by this patient and her family who wanted to be catered to in a manner that the staff believed bordered on entitlement. From the staff's perspective, a blue-collar family was "sticking it" to them, demanding to be waited on. Pride became a feature of the dynamic. In feeling duped, clinicians believed that their status was being reduced and that they were not being treated with the respect that they deserved. Not wanting to be made to look foolish or weak, the clinicians sought to exert power, to have the patient removed from the unit, forced to get her care elsewhere.

Clearly pride was interfering with reason. Emotion Mind activation was obscuring more rational assessments of what else might be going on. Attempts to dig deeper had been usurped by efforts to appease clinician feelings of exploitation. Strong emotions, collectively reinforced by the groupthink mentality of the health care team, served only to solidify the team's negative judgment. As the weeks went on, staff sentiment grew more hostile and outside intervention became necessary.

Had Reason Mind been summoned and compassion activated, a more accurate assessment of the situation could have been obtained. As it turned out, Marsha was married to a man of whom her parents strongly disapproved. Having grown up in a strict, religious household, Marsha, who met her husband at a church-sponsored retreat, fell in love with his zest for life, his love of music and dance, his charming demeanor, and his promises of a more exciting life. Given her religious beliefs, her attraction to him could only be fulfilled through marriage, so she and Billy married 6 months after they met, in spite of her parent's strong objections. At the time, Marsha was 19, attending college, and working part-time. Billy was unemployed, dabbled in recreational drugs, and had no identifiable means of support. After 2 years, Billy remained unable to keep a job for more than a few weeks at a time and had relied on Marsha's meager salary to finance ill-conceived, get-rich-quick schemes, forcing Marsha to drop out of college and work full time. When trying to seek support and counsel from her parents, Marsha was met with an angry, "we-told-you-so" attitude and a reminder that marriage was a lifelong commitment, for better or worse. While feeling trapped and overwhelmed, without support or resources, Marsha discovered she was pregnant. Not wanting to raise the child in such a dysfunctional marriage, but terrified at the thought of trying to make it on her own, she contemplated divorce, and thought to use what was left of her meager savings to cover expenses during the baby's first year. It was only then that she discovered that Billy had cleaned out the savings account, just weeks before, in order to fund a recent drug binge. Her nausea intensified, and a few weeks later her vomiting was so severe that she was unable to work and her mother insisted Marsha move back home and be cared for by her parents. This was an offer that

Marsha had not anticipated, and she was relieved to have a viable option for support but realized the truce with her parents would likely disintegrate if she lost the pregnancy. The vomiting made Marsha very anxious. She saw it as a threat to bringing the fetus to term. She wondered if God was punishing her for leaving her husband. She felt guilty, unlovable, and defeated. The hospital provided temporary respite from the consequences of her impulsive, immature, and deleterious life choices. It also served, at least in her mind, as the only hope of controlling the vomiting and carrying the baby to term. But as the staff turned against her, her feelings of unworthiness and guilt increased and the vomiting worsened.

Was Marsha's nausea and vomiting aggravated by anxiety? Likely so. Was it solely anxiety induced? Likely not. Although some of her thought processes were distorted or unsophisticated, it was clear that she was not feigning illness in order to dupe staff or exploit resources. But the contagion of suspicion among the staff had become so pervasive that, eventually, few of the providers were able to transcend their own biases enough to form any rapport with the patient. With each encounter, the situation worsened, defensiveness mounted on both sides, and there was no space left for trust to develop and for Marsha's story to emerge. It was only with the intervention of an objective outsider that more of the context of Marsha's condition came to light.

Did the obstetrical staff lack basic compassion? Were they an unusual assortment of nurses and physicians who regularly gang up on working-class patients? To the contrary, these were a committed group of clinicians who prided themselves in providing the highest-quality care. So how is it that an "us-versus-them" mentality could so easily obstruct a patient's care? A collective, tacit agreement to avoid self-reflection seems to be at the core. Something about this case tapped into a deep need for what the staff seemed to think was a restoration of justice. Somehow feeling as if they were being duped provoked strong feelings of resistance to what the staff saw as the family's efforts to play out dynamics of dominance and subordination—a working-class family sticking it to the system. And although misguided assumptions were clearly at play, few if any of the staff were willing to take a look at those assumptions and suggest alternate perspectives. It was as if any dissenter, by expressing doubt at the team's conclusion, would be considered disloyal to the group's effort to demand justice. Strong social forces were at play, keeping individuals from engaging in exactly the kind of self-reflection that is so necessary in these situations. Sometimes the sense of belonging that comes with solidarity is so seductive that even the most compassionate among us can become blinded.

Strong emotions, unexamined, can obscure the judgment of even seasoned professionals. Without the capacity to step back and become an observer of our emotional state, it is difficult to gain perspective. Left unexamined, emotions can then drive our behaviors in ways that reflect more primitive modes of operation. Stepping back to deliberately search for and discover hidden feelings borne of erroneous assumptions brings those biases to light. Once discovered, these assumptions can be challenged, and imposing reason can offer counterbalances against the force of these biased perspectives and prompt wiser thinking. But in all of it, we have to be willing—willing to stop, look, listen, and feel those inner workings of emotional reactivity. We must be willing to search for and label those emotions, consider their impact, and honor their value, but more critically consider whether acting from them is warranted. We must be willing to hold our emotions up against scrutiny to see if they might be exaggerated or unfounded, based on faulty assumptions or misinterpretations of the truth. We have to be willing to embrace the deep benefits of humility, to accept that, as humans, we will be misled at times by emotions that, although important and valuable, sometimes lead us astray. We need to be willing to accept that emotions are not always warranted or justified, and we need to be willing to catch ourselves and summon up the courage to self-correct.

Workplace conflict is inevitable, no matter whether the work occurs in a small family-owned business, a major corporation, or in health care. From children making sand castles to surgeons removing tumors, individuals will hold varying perspectives on the most appropriate and efficient method for getting the job done. In health care, these perspectives can vary considerably. But within health care, the stakes are high. The tone and flavor of our disagreements can have a significant impact on patient care quality and safety.

Even within a given discipline, opinions can vary markedly. The trauma surgeon attempting to manage the immediate postoperative care of a patient with delirium may vehemently disagree with the psychiatrist who refuses to transfer the patient to her inpatient unit for care. Each is convinced that the patient will be better managed on the other's respective service. Surgeons can operate from a place of believing that they are the "real" doctors, the experts, and the ones who are in charge and that their colleagues in psychiatry are less rigorously trained. Psychiatrists may regard surgeons as bullying tyrants, determined to have things go their own way.

Nurses working to manage difficult patient behaviors can become equally entrenched in their personal perspectives. Even nurses working together in the same specialty may disagree about how best to manage the demanding patient who is consistently ringing the call bell and asking for assistance with activities that do not require professional nursing assistance. One of the nurses is convinced that by all of the nurses agreeing to meet the patient's inappropriate requests with a stern and withholding demeanor, the patient will be forced to act differently. Her opposing colleague believes that through calm, gentle, and consistent support, the patient's anxiety will dissipate and with it, her demands for inappropriate attention will cease. Different strategies and different opinions are pervasive within health care.

Not only are professionals educated from sometimes very different conceptual models of care, but they also are educated from very different professional socialization processes. Physicians are often taught to see themselves as the best educated and the most knowledgeable of their health care team colleagues. They assume roles as team leaders, as authority figures, and as the people who direct the care. Nurses are socialized to see themselves as facilitators of patient and family adaptation, the ones who monitor the patient's responses to changing illness manifestations, detect nuances in patient health status, and act quickly to address critical needs. Nurses see themselves as the front-line deliverers of essential, often lifesaving care and as critical patient and family advocates. Nurses assess shifting stages of recovery, attend to psychosocial needs, and come to understand not only the illness but the patient and family experiencing that illness. Social workers facilitate patient discharge, provide additional support, access sources of funding, and connect patients to important resources that can help patients more successfully transition from hospital to the home. Respiratory therapists, physical therapists, and others play important roles in addressing patients' needs and moving patients from illness to recovery. Although conflict between professional colleagues occurs within and between all professional groups, conflicts among and between nurses and physicians are common.

Christy Myers, MD, and Jeff Carter, RN, are working with Mrs. Bartholomew (Mrs. B), a 75-year-old widow who has breast cancer that is not responding to the third course of chemotherapy. Dr. Myers's goal for today's encounter is to share with Mrs. B that the only aggressive treatment option left is to enroll her in a clinical trial with a new chemotherapy medication under development. Mr. Carter's position is that these new medications offer slim chance of providing a significant benefit to Mrs. B, and are much more likely to make her remaining months very uncomfortable with unpredictable and painful side effects.

Christy Myers is fond of Mrs. B and has been working with her for 2 years. She is apprehensive about having to share the news and is feeling the need to provide Mrs. B with some kind of hope. Jeff Carter, less familiar with Mrs. B, is focused on Mrs. B receiving accurate information about the hazards of clinical trials and realizes that his role is, in part, to support Mrs. B through the emotional distress she is likely to experience as a result of learning that she is terminally ill.

Both clinicians are well intentioned and are concerned about Mrs. B's well-being. Christy's desire to provide hope meets a need in Mrs. B but also a need within Christy. Telling a patient that she is dying is a very distressing task. Christy feels that on some level, she has let Mrs. B down—she has failed to meet the patient's expectations for cure. Christy's unexamined and unidentified emotions could easily get in the way of her message. In fact, she may end up painting a rosier picture of the benefits of the experimental drug to

Mrs. B because she doesn't want to feel her own emotional suffering at having to provide bad news. Although her emotions are completely understandable, it is in the patient's best interest for Christy to remain mindful of whose needs are actually being served: the patient's or the physician's (in this case, it is likely a bit of both).

Jeff may be in a better position to remain objective. He too cares about Mrs. B and wants to be present to provide emotional support, but he realizes that by glossing over the details of Mrs. B's terminal state and instilling false hope, Christy could ultimately be doing Mrs. B more harm than good. By offering a treatment option that is much more likely to be detrimental than helpful, Christy is inadvertently doing harm. He believes that Christy's best course of action is to compassionately provide accurate information and then allow the patient to express her grief, difficult as that may be on all three of them. By providing honest and accurate information, Jeff believes that he and Christy have an opportunity to help Mrs. B through the grieving process and then ultimately to help the patient make appropriate and important plans for the time she has left. He has less history with this patient, and less of a sense of having failed her, and therefore feels little of the angst that plagues Christy. He also has little knowledge of the specific chemo agent that Christy is recommending. This makes him more certain that his perspective on clinical trials is correct and that his own motives are clear. However, he has struggled with physicians in the past, feeling that his female nurse peers are remiss in their obligation to question the treatment decisions of their physician colleagues. Jeff feels that he must act as a strong patient advocate, especially in the kinds of situations where a patient's journey toward a peaceful death could be sabotaged by uncomfortable and futile chemotherapy. Because he has taken this on as a mission, he fails to recognize that sometimes he comes across with a kind of self-righteousness that makes his colleagues recoil.

Too often, well-meaning clinicians are oblivious to the extent to which their own needs influence their thinking and judgment. Emotional distress is a powerful force, especially dangerous when left undetected and unexamined. Christy might justify the clinical trial option with rationales like the following: "I want to give the patient every possible chance at survival, and even though it's a long shot, we need to give it a try," or "I don't want to take away all of her hope. Without hope Mrs. B won't be able to cope," or "I'm an oncologist, and my job is to try every means of fighting the cancer." But these thoughts, although often powerful and well meaning, can sit in an isolated corner in Christy's consciousness, away from Reason Mind's scrutiny, and therefore in a protected place where, left uncovered, they can serve to help Christy avoid the physical and emotional discomfort that scrutiny may bring. The possibility that the treatment she is proposing may offer only harm and no benefit may be too disturbing for Christy to think about. If other oncologists support a similar, less rigorous appraisal of the value of clinical trials, Dr. M may obtain group-based reinforcement for keeping scrutiny at bay.

At the same time, because of Jeff's belief that clinical trials serve only to advance science and that few if any patients actually benefit, he too may be reflexively operating from a faulty belief. His opinion regarding Mrs. B's care may be based more on his own need to act in concert with his belief than to objectively consider the relative merits of the current investigational drug. Without mindful consideration, he could fall into the trap of assuming that all clinical trials are the same, and that every patient who participates in one is merely a physician's guinea pig. And if the clinical trial being considered is in the third phase of investigation and has a strong likelihood of helping Mrs. B, then Jeff's position could serve only to undermine, rather than enhance, Mrs. B's care.

If Jeff approaches Christy from a position of self-righteous indignation at her decision to offer a clinical trial option to Mrs. B, and Christy responds to Jeff with anger and prideful entitlement, insulted by what she interprets as a challenge to her authority, then they complicate matters even more. Each is responding to the other with considerable emotional baggage. In this battle for power and control, the patient's well-being can become secondary. Egos can so dominate these scuffles that important patient care considerations can get lost.

Scrutiny and mindfulness are critical to avoiding such skirmishes and/or nipping them in the bud. Mindful practices help clinicians better identify emotional minefields and keep better track of whose needs are being served. Interdisciplinary dialog and team-based care management are essential for effective coordinated patient care. Disagreements are much better managed when they can be openly, respectfully, and nondefensively addressed. All members of the health care team provide valuable input into care decisions and all perspectives need to be solicited and valued in order for patient quality and safety efforts to be most effective. Unexamined treatment decisions can result in patients being harmed rather than healed. If our ultimate goal is to, wherever possible, consistently reduce suffering, then a commitment to mindfulness facilitates a kind of vigilance, a willingness to question, again and again, what purpose is being pursued, what goals are being met, and whose interests are being served. Mindfulness is a form of critical thinking, a process of metacognition, where the clinician is actually thinking about his or her thinking. Moving through a mindfulness-based examination of her own thinking processes, Christy could utilize a structure, or template, that looks something like this:

1. What do I want for Mrs. B?
2. What does Mrs. B want for herself? Do I know? Does she value quality of life over quantity of life?
3. What are my primary (cure, when cure is possible) and secondary (support and end-of-life management, when cure is not) roles in this situation?
4. What does Mrs. B expect of me?
5. What do I expect of myself?
6. What are my feelings and concerns about having to give Mrs. B bad news?
7. What are my fears about the impact this news might have on Mrs. B?
8. How might my own feelings, needs, and concerns influence the manner in which I approach this encounter?
9. How does my professional bias influence my thinking? What alternative perspectives might I—in the name of objectivity—offer the patient?
10. How much of my own distress about Mrs. B's illness is entering into my thinking?
11. What demeanor should I assume in order to be most effective?
12. What would "effectiveness" look like in this situation?
13. What perspectives do my health care colleagues hold about this situation? How might their perspectives better guide my treatment opinions?

14. How do I convey respect and regard for the opinions of my colleagues, even if I don't always agree with them? I need to be open to their ideas and less engaged in defending my own position.
15. I need to remember that the highest-quality patient care comes from professionals working together, communicating openly, and welcoming different ideas.

Jeff's list of self-assessment questions might look very similar but with a few modifications:

1. What do I want for Mrs. B?
2. What does Mrs. B want for herself? Do I know? Does she value quality of life over quantity of life?
3. What are my primary and secondary roles in this situation?
4. What does Mrs. B expect of me?
5. What do I expect of myself?
6. What are my feelings and concerns about having to support Mrs. B after she receives the bad news?
7. What are my fears about the impact this news might have on Mrs. B, and will I have the time to give her the emotional support she needs and deserves?
8. How might my own feelings, needs, and concerns influence the manner in which I approach this encounter?
9. What kinds of professional or personal bias might I bring into this situation?
10. How much of my own distress about Mrs. B being given accurate information is entering into my thinking?
11. What demeanor should I assume in order to be most effective?
12. What would "effectiveness" look like in this situation?

13. What perspectives do my health care colleagues hold about this situation? How might their perspectives better guide my treatment opinions?

14. How do I convey respect and regard for the opinions of my colleagues, even if I don't always agree with them? I need to be open to their ideas and less engaged in defending my own position.

15. I need to remember that the highest-quality patient care comes from professionals working together, communicating openly, and welcoming different ideas.

Substance Abuse

Substance abuse is a significant health problem. Patients who struggle with substance abuse bear considerable risk for multiple physical, psychological, and social sequelae. All of this is compounded by the negative attitudes that these patients regularly experience from health care providers. Just like people who are thought to be feigning illness (see Chapter 17: Somatic Complaints), those who abuse substances are often blamed for their condition and are considered undeserving of empathy and attention. In fact, rather than compassion, substance-abusing patients can experience outright hostility from providers who believe that, in essence, through stupidity and self-indulgence, these patients have created their own suffering. In our politically correct workplaces, much of this hostility now goes underground, but highly disparaging terms are still used in informal interactions among colleagues when describing substance-abusing patients.

To the uninformed, addiction *can* look like little more than a person's deliberate selection of a hedonistic lifestyle, but for most of the people caught in its grip, addiction is a constant struggle to try to transcend the pull of (albeit destructive) relief from the pain of a frustrating, chaotic, existence.

Clinical Example

Buddy Hughes was born to a 16-year-old mother who had run away from her abusive family and was living with an aunt in a housing project in a major city. During his early years, Buddy's mother, Sue, worked long days as a housekeeper in a local hotel, but was home at night to help with homework. His great-aunt Hazel was disabled from a factory accident but was available in the daytime, providing the kind of supportive supervision that is critical to a child's sense of well-being. His mother and great-aunt were very protective of Buddy and had strict rules about him doing well in school and helping out at home. Then, when Buddy was 12 years old, Hazel died suddenly of a heart attack. He and Sue now had to fend for themselves. Sue, still gone much of the day and often working double shifts, regrettably left Buddy to come home after school to an empty apartment. Feeling lonely and isolated, Buddy began to break the rules and venture outside, looking for companionship. He found an older peer, who took an interest in Buddy and began to expose him to a side of life that, up until then, Buddy had rarely seen. Buddy quickly discovered that his neighborhood was filled with substance abuse. He became much more aware of the neighbors and community members who were either abusing or dealing drugs; it was the norm in his neighborhood.

Before long his newfound friend was encouraging Buddy to "act like a man," to take risks, to rail against rules and limits and experiment with the drugs and alcohol that were readily available. The social pressure proved to be too much and Buddy found himself giving in to the taunts to smoke crack and guzzle the cheap wine that almost everyone in the projects seemed to be drinking. When his mother discovered what was happening, she relocated them, moving to a different neighborhood and enrolling Buddy in a new school. But this was a tough move for his mom. Feeling isolated from her old friends, and without the company of her favorite aunt, she fell into a pattern of drinking alcohol after work, and was often drunk by the time bedtime arrived. Buddy finished high school and did relatively well until being laid off from his construction job after the downturn in the economy. Finding alternate employment was difficult, given his limited skills. Seeing how hard his mother had worked and how little she had to show for it only served to fuel his sense of resentment and frustration. By this time his mother had fully succumbed to the lure of alcohol and was living in squalor in an efficiency apartment and receiving public assistance. Buddy was living with friends who partied frequently and spent most weekends drinking and sometimes experimenting with drugs. During the time period when he was consistently employed, Buddy was able to avoid joining in: He simply ignored their invitations to participate. But without a job and with an increasing sense of anger and worthlessness, his resolve dissipated. As a relationship with a long-term girlfriend disintegrated and as Buddy's demeanor became more sullen, it became harder and harder for him to avoid the pull of substance-based relief. It was soon after the girlfriend left him that Buddy found himself alone, unemployed, depressed, and taking advantage of every opportunity to soothe his distress by partying with his friends. He was especially drawn to the mood-elevating effects of cocaine. Because cocaine was too expensive for regular use, Buddy looked into crystal methamphetamine as a cheaper, more available alternative. With a recipe he'd found on the Internet, Buddy concocted some crystal meth, which provided effective, if temporary, relief from his depression, at a fraction of the cost of crack. Seeing just how effective it was, and realizing that he could make some money selling it to others, he decided to rent a dilapidated farm on the very edges of the city and set up his own meth lab. His addiction in full bloom, he deteriorated quickly. An explosion in the lab brought Buddy to the attention of the health care system when he was admitted to the local hospital for treatment of extensive burns. Results from a urine toxicology screen revealed his addiction.

Not every person who grows up in poverty or in an inner-city housing project becomes a drug dealer. But exposure to drugs early in life, especially in environments where relief from emotional pain is commonly obtained through abuse of substances, imprints ideas for coping. In families or communities where substance abuse is the "norm," an individual's risk for substance abuse is far greater than in areas where drug use is rare or nonexistent. In times of trouble, we all look for solace, often in methods or through channels that are most familiar to us. We tend to gravitate to means commonly used by the people around us. If we are exposed to people who cope constructively, who talk through their concerns with trusted friends, who gather advice and insight from wise mentors, who draw from family and neighbors and clergy soothing love and support, then effective coping skills are well known to us. We are more likely to imitate these coping skills to deal with adversity because we've witnessed how well such skills have worked for those around us. But if we've had little exposure to constructive coping, we know little of the methods. If our world is filled with people who feel beaten down and depressed, who themselves have shallow reserves of emotional energy from which others can draw support, who have little hope to offer and no expertise from which to construct sound advice, then how can we be expected to know that constructive coping methods actually exist? We learn to address adversity by imitating the coping efforts, effective or ineffective, of the people who surround us, and in Buddy's case, he has witnessed that hard work does not produce economic success and that most people cope with loneliness, depression, and despair with drugs and alcohol.

In mindfulness-based practice, the clinician sees Buddy not as a "dirtbag" but as a person caught up in a series of unfortunate circumstances. The nurse understands that Buddy's reactions to his life circumstances, although admittedly impulsive or shortsighted, have served as a familiar means of meeting an intense need. Because his life has exposed him to few alternatives, Buddy has met his needs by mimicking patterns he has consistently witnessed in his environment. Although Buddy's life choices may trigger strong negative emotions in the clinicians assigned to his care, such emotions do not have to *dictate* his care. If his clinicians can begin to acknowledge that although their own emotions are strong and are based on important values, and that these values are based in what the clinicians believe is good/bad, right/wrong, then there is an opportunity for the clinicians to shift to Reason Mind thinking. And once in Reason Mind, the clinicians can quickly redirect their focus to "just the facts." The fact is that Buddy has been exposed to difficult circumstances where the people in his life have turned to drugs and alcohol, often as a means to escape from feelings of depression and hopelessness. His clinicians, college graduates with the advantage of education and opportunity, more likely come from families where education was valued and the family home was located in a place of relative safety and security, where drugs may have been available but were not the common method chosen by parents and neighbors to cope with life's adversities. The clinician operating from Reason Mind has an opportunity to acknowledge that life experiences have an enormous impact on how we all learn to cope and that most of us in health care have had the advantages of intelligence, family support, and education to guide our life's journey in a constructive direction.

In Wise Mind, the clinician can begin to ease into the idea that Buddy is a product of negative life events and that those events and circumstances have shaped him. In Wise Mind the clinician might begin to have insight into the notion that everyone is not born into the same advantages. Advantage is difficult to see when we are in the midst of it. Growing up in an environment where we feel safe, have enough resources to meet our basic human needs, are loved and valued, and have role models that demonstrate the ability to cope effectively with life's hardships without the need to escape via drugs and alcohol confers profound advantage. Buddy's mother did the best she could under the circumstances, but in spite of her best efforts, Buddy has been exposed to ineffective coping methods that are part of the culture of his world. No wonder he found himself following this same path.

In Wise Mind the clinician approaches Buddy from a position of nonjudgment. To "observe and describe without judgment" is critical to being able to extend to the patient a gesture of understanding and acceptance. Acceptance isn't about approving of the patient's lifestyle; it is about accepting that right here, right now, this is where the patient is, and as clinicians, it is our job to see how we might offer help and support, conveying our belief that change is possible and Buddy has innate intrinsic value. He is worth our best efforts.

Clinical Scenario

Jessica Witherspoon suffers from vascular migraine headaches. These headaches tend to occur every 6 months or so, when she is under time-pressured work stress. For the past 4 weeks Jessica has been working on developing a grant. Her university position requires that she obtain grant funding to support her research. She is aware that her viability for tenure is dependent on successfully securing such funding, but the federal agencies that provide grants have scarce dollars to award, making the grant submission process more competitive than ever before. Jessica has been working long days and nights, collaborating with other members of her research team, consulting with other colleagues, and spending 16-hour days at the computer. Although she is aware that lack of sleep and poor eating increase her risk of migraine, she is frantic to submit her grant on time. The grant is due before midnight on Wednesday. It is Sunday evening and Jessica has been battling a migraine since before dawn this morning. The pain has been increasing all day and now her head feels like it is going to explode. She is writhing in pain on the bathroom floor, lifting her head only long enough to vomit into the toilet about every 20 minutes. Her eyes pulsate with pain every time she looks at her computer screen, or any source of bright light. Her husband is angry with her for becoming so obsessed with work, and resentful that her work is keeping her from meeting her parenting obligations for their 9-year-old son. But he also knows that these headaches can last for 48 hours or longer, and the longer it lasts, the more behind Jessica will get and the more anxious she will become. He insists that she go to the emergency department (ED) and have her headache treated. He has phoned her sister and asked her to come and take Jessica to the ED—he will stay home with their son.

At the ED, Jessica is questioned by the triage nurse who attempts to obtain a brief history of Jessica's migraine. He then explains that victims from a multivehicle accident are currently being treated and the wait time is likely to be over an hour. Two hours pass as Jessica and her sister sit anxiously in the waiting area while Jessica has episodes of dry heaving. When she is finally seen, Jessica is irritable, agitated, in agony, and dehydrated. The ED physician approaches her curtly and asks her to rate her pain on a 1-to-10 scale. When she tells him it's a "10," he rolls his eyes. As he leaves her cubicle, Jessica overhears him saying to a colleague "Yeah, a 10, that's what they all say. Give me a break! It looks like we've got another drug seeker looking to us to score her next fix." The nurse comes in next and, having heard the physician's suspicion, interviews the patient in an emotionally distant and business-like manner: "When did you say the pain started? How long do your migraines usually last? How do the migraines usually resolve if you don't come to the ED for pain medication?" The nurse suggests to the patient that because the patient's migraines usually last from 12 to 24 hours, and at this point, it has already been over 16 hours since onset, perhaps the patient should just wait it out until the migraine passes. Jessica is now furious and demands to be treated. The nurse then interprets the demand as just the kind of rude and entitled behavior typical of "drug-seeking" patients.

Practice Considerations

In the typical ED situation, clinicians have little information about the context of a patient's pain experience. Their
assessments usually focus on the symptoms themselves,
and exploring possible underlying pathology. The facts
about Jessica's life, work demands, and general personality remain unknown to ED personnel. It is easy for such
personnel to use stereotyped beliefs to back-fill information gaps to form a complete, if erroneous, picture of the
patient. In this case, they've determined that Jessica is a
substance-abusing patient determined to manipulate them
into providing unwarranted medication.

It is true that, at times, people desperate for substances
to ease their addiction come to EDs for relief. It is also true
that ED personnel often feel abused, manipulated, and
duped when these situations happen and they respond
from an emotional position of being deeply insulted. This
response, although understandable, is not very effective in
meeting the needs of either the patient or the provider.

In Jessica's case, the jaded physician has, through
suggestion, also created suspicion in the mind of the
nurse, and the prejudice communicated to Jessica is deeply
disturbing to her. This is the antithesis of therapeutic,
healing and compassionate care.

Questions

1. How could an exploration of Reason Mind principles
   have helped the physician to offer a more compassionate approach to Jessica?

2. What Body Mind experiences might he have been having prior to and during his initial encounter with her (consider fatigue, frustration, sore feet, hunger, etc.)?

3. Given what you know about the conditions within the ED that evening, what Emotion Mind phenomena may have been activated in the staff both before and during this encounter with Jessica?

4. What mindfulness-based practices could have been used, by both the physician and the nurse, to enhance the encounter with Jessica?

5. Given that EDs are high-stress environments, what regular mindfulness practices might help the staff better cope and offer more compassionate care to patients?

Cultivating Mindfulness

20

Throughout this book, mindfulness has been recommended as the scaffolding upon which clinicians can consistently engage patients in therapeutic encounters and build a compassionate practice. Mindfulness provides a framework for monitoring our emotions and examining our thoughts as we move through our professional lives. But for mindfulness to become a way of life, deliberate and consistent practice is required. For many people, that practice is fostered through meditation. Some readers may recoil at this last sentence and cringe at the notion of meditation, thinking that it represents the practice of an Eastern religion and, as such, opposes Christianity, Judaism, and/or Islam. To the contrary, meditation is a cognitive practice (Siegel, 2010) where the goal is to focus the mind and foster the capacity to remain centered in the present moment, here and now, rather than be ruminating about the past or worrying about the future. Meditation does not contradict any religious doctrine or promote any notion of a deity. It is, instead, a deliberate effort to develop a stronger capacity to focus attention and subsequently achieve a state of equilibrium. It is a matter of sitting quietly and redirecting thoughts back to the present moment. Many people do this through focusing on their breathing. Others practice walking meditation or yoga as methods that help to keep attention focused on the present moment and on the immediate sensations within the body. For those unfamiliar with such practices, they can sound not only unconventional, but also trendy, faddish, or even ridiculous. Sitting still for 10 minutes and focusing on one's breath might appear to be a pointless exercise. Yet there is research to suggest that by doing just that, the brain develops neural pathways that, during times of stress, allow us to more easily access centers of calm and equanimity.

Emotional activation can result in habitual responses that we fall into thoughtlessly. These are just the times when we most need to operate from a calm, even-tempered center. In the face of difficult patient encounters, when our own anxiety and distress might tempt us to resort to self-serving methods of escaping or avoiding such encounters, we can more easily enter a place of calm centeredness in order to deal with the situation more effectively. Meditation, then, is the means to an end, not an end in itself. Through meditation, we can more easily shift into calm centeredness, a state of balanced equilibrium that allows us to achieve a more tranquil state, more able to strategically think through the steps of mindful patient care. With equanimity it is easier to assess our Emotion Mind influences (anxiety, fear, annoyance, urgency) to scan our Body Mind for physical manifestations of stress (tightened jaw, knotted stomach, flustered movements, or even pain or hunger) and to move into Reason Mind and consider the facts of the situation. Having examined our mind states, we can then deliberately enter Wise Mind to synthesize the data and formulate an effective course of action. In Wise

Mind, we can more easily consider the thoughts, feelings, and needs of patients and families and strategize how best to meet these. (Author's note: Several no-cost apps are now available that provide instruction in the fundamentals of meditation. One to consider is The Mindful Revolution series within The Mindfulness Training App.)

Measuring Mindfulness

The Mindfulness Attention Awareness Scale (Brown, n.d.; Brown & Ryan, 2003) can be used to help identify habits of mind that interfere with being right here, right now. The scale can be accessed at www.ppc.sas.upenn.edu/mindfulnessscale .pdf, and scoring guidelines are provided. Using this scale, perhaps on a weekly basis, might be useful in tracking our capacity to become progressively more mindful and may be helpful in prompting more deliberate mindful activity.

Mindful Activities and Practices

Several techniques enhance mindfulness and mindful practice:

- Make the practice of self-reflection, of looking inward from an observer's perspective, a habit.
  - Do this, perhaps every day, as a way of centering and preparing to start the day.
- Observe and describe emotions, thoughts, and sensations without judging them.
  - Notice them. Identify them. Assess and examine them.

- Hold up long-held assumptions to scrutiny, noting biases and stereotypes.
  - This is especially difficult and takes humility and almost constant surveillance.
- Challenge biases. Learn more about people's ways and beliefs. Act from a more objective perspective.
  - Take on an attitude of acceptance of others.
- Do one thing at a time, deliberately, and with full attention.
  - Accept the myth of multitasking and do one thing, then the next.
- Be fully present in even routine activities such as washing dishes.
  - Catch worries and expectations as they come and go and bring attention back to the present moment, fully experiencing the tactile and visual features of the activity.
- Engage in relaxation techniques (see the resources at the websites noted at the end of this chapter).
  - Listen to a progressive relaxation program, take a walk, or have a cup of tea.
  - Breathe, deep and slow. (Use this one multiple times a day.)
- Decide to do the opposite of our usual reflexive, but less effective, behaviors.
  - After a stressful day, instead of isolating, go be with friends.
- Practice assertiveness when assertiveness is warranted.
  - Respectfully state your position and ask that it be considered.
- Stay with a difficult emotion, rather than escaping it or distracting yourself from it, so that its power to elicit fear can be diminished.

■ Stay with the angry patient and tolerate your initial discomfort, accepting rather than resisting the anger, and calmly convey that acceptance to the patient.

These and many other techniques are described at the following websites:

www.getselfhelp.co.ukmindfulness.htm
www.dbtselfhelp.com.htm

And at the following two apps:

The Mindfulness Training App
Stop, Breathe & Think

References

Brown, K. W. (n.d.). *Mindfulness Attention Awareness Scale.* Retrieved January 24, 2014, from http://www.ppc.sas.upenn .edu/mindfulnessscale.pdf

Brown, K. W., & Ryan, R. M. (2003). The benefits of being present: Mindfulness and its role in psychological well-being. *Journal of Personality and Social Psychology, 84*(4), 822–848. doi: 10.1037/ 0022-3514.84.4.822

Siegel, D. J. (2010). *Mindsight: The new science of personal transformation* (1st ed.). New York, NY: Bantam Books.

Index